GERMAN COOKING

GERMAN COOKING

by
ROBIN HOWE

ANDRE DEUTSCH

FIRST PUBLISHED FEBRUARY 1953 BY
ANDRE DEUTSCH LIMITED
105 GREAT RUSSELL STREET
LONDON WC1

REVISED AND ENLARGED EDITION SEPTEMBER 1954
EIGHTH IMPRESSION JUNE 1975
FIRST PAPERBACK EDITION JANUARY 1983

ISBN 0 233 97583 7

CONTENTS

CONVERSION TABLES (APPROXIMATE)

FROM IMPERIAL TO METRIC MEASURES

WEIGHTS

Imperial	Metric
$\frac{1}{4}$oz	$7\frac{1}{2}$–8g
$\frac{1}{2}$oz	15g
1oz	30g
4oz ($\frac{1}{4}$lb)	110g
8oz ($\frac{1}{2}$lb)	225g
16oz (1lb)	450g
$1\frac{1}{2}$lb	675g
5lb	2.3 kilos

LIQUID MEASURES

	ml	fl.oz
$1\frac{3}{4}$ pints	1000 (1 litre)	35
1 pint	570	20
$\frac{3}{4}$ pint	425	15
$\frac{1}{2}$ pint	290	10
$\frac{1}{3}$ pint	190	6·6
$\frac{1}{4}$ pint (1 gill)	150	5
	56	2
2 scant tablespoons	28	1
1 teaspoon	5	

USEFUL MEASUREMENTS

1 egg	56ml/2 fl.oz
1 egg white	28ml/1 fl.oz
1 rounded tablespoon flour	30g/1oz
1 rounded tablespoon cornflour	30g/1oz
1 rounded tablespoon sugar	30g/1oz
2 rounded tablespoons breadcrumbs	30g/1oz
2 level teaspoons gelatine	8g/$\frac{1}{4}$oz

INTRODUCTION

GERMANS are hearty eaters, and their meals are substantial. They love dumplings: thick, warming soups: meat and sausages: heavy, dark breads and vegetables of all kinds. Like the French they love their food and have firm, if sometimes unorthodox, ideas on the subject.

As Germany is a unit consisting of several countries it is obvious much of its cooking must be regional. The German from Silesia will have entirely different ideas of what is good to eat from the German from Hamburg or Munich. Even some of the names are different. A potato, for example, in the north is a *Kartoffel*, while in the south it becomes an *Erdapfel*.

At first glance some combinations in German cooking may cause the average housewife in this country to raise an eyebrow. But once they have been tried they seem natural enough.

The Germans are very fond of 'bitter-sweet' mixtures, such as apples with potatoes, or pork with dried fruits. A marinade of wine vinegar, raisins, sugar and lemon juice produces a distinctive flavour. Red cabbage is cooked with apples and onions, and in Bavaria diced fried bacon is sometimes added. Sauerkraut, that favourite of German vegetables, is boiled with carraway seeds; shrimps and mushrooms are often used as garnishes together.

Particularly interesting is the German method of cooking vegetables. Many years ago vegetables were almost always creamed, but nowadays there is less creaming. Even so they are generally tossed in a little butter before water is added and the vegetables left to simmer until tender. Many of their vegetable dishes are a meal in themselves.

Although one might feel that German cooking with its heavy demands on butter, eggs, mushrooms, flavourings, etc, is extravagant, nothing is ever wasted. The ends of asparagus are used for soups and not thrown away as so often is the case in this country. The giblets, etc, of the traditional Christmas goose are turned into a delicacy famed all over Germany. The liver is fried with apples and onions, and anything still left over forms the basis for a soup.

From the North Sea coast and their numerous rivers, the Germans receive their full quota of fish. Here again they use original methods of cooking. Especially attractive is the way of cooking fish 'blue'. When freshly caught trout is prepared in this way it has a flavour which is quite unforgettable. Herrings probably get the finest treatment in the world in Germany. Certainly they are not treated as shabbily as they are in our own country. In North Germany the humble herring becomes the king of fish.

A book could be written on dumplings alone. They are made with meat and without; sweet and sour; with eggs and flour, and with cottage cheese. They are baked, fried, poached and boiled; they appear in soups, stews, pies, and served with stewed fruit. There are even tiny meringue dumplings for the fruit soups so favoured in summer.

Soups are popular in all parts of Germany. In the north they favour thick soups and fruit soups. The latter are usually made from apples or soft fruit. Wine and beer soups also win favour in the north. The south appears to prefer thin, clear soups, adding sago or semolina, noodles or thin strips of cooked pancakes.

The German day starts early with 'first' breakfast. This usually consists of coffee and a roll, or a slice of rye bread spread with butter. Second breakfast is about ten-thirty and is often quite a large meal. Promptly at this time in offices all over Germany sandwiches, thick and appetising, are taken out of the inevitable despatch case and eaten.

In most homes, wherever possible, the main meal of the day is the mid-day one. It is usually hot and substantial. Many homes have now instituted the 'five o'clock tea' habit which consists either of milkless tea or coffee with whipped cream and cakes. The Germans excel in cake making and it is difficult for anyone, even on the most rigid diet, to refuse a slice of some of their wonderful *Torten.*

In the evening the housewife produces a light casserole dish and follows this with a large plate of mixed cold cuts. These range from raw ham to the many delightful sausages so beloved by the Germans. Or she may produce instead a plate of open sandwiches. Here she uses her imagination. Salads will accompany these, and the sandwiches will be eaten with a knife and fork. In most cases a bottle of wine is there to help wash down the meal.

Cheese almost always follows the last meal of the day.

In compiling this book I have adapted the recipes as little as possible, in order to retain their German character, but have tried to choose those dishes most suited to this country, and to give a representative collection. If more come from the north than the south, that is easily explained as I spent more time in the north.

What I have hoped to do is to help bring variety to the British table, for there is a great deal of good eating in Germany.

I have made a few corrections and alterations to the text for this second edition of *German Cooking*, which will, I hope, improve it; and I have taken the opportunity to add a number of new recipes.

ROBIN HOWE

SOUPS

Soups in Germany are probably more varied than in any other country. Apart from the heavy warming soups, particularly appreciated in the north, there are the famous fruit soups from Hamburg. These are eaten in the summer, and should precede the meal. In Berlin wine, beer and elderberry soup is especially popular, although to the non-German these soups are very much an acquired taste, especially when they are warm and have macaroon biscuits floating on the top. Popular all over the country are clear soups, to which have been added small liver or meat dumplings, sago or semolina or thin strips of egg custard, which has been baked so firm that it can be shaped into stars, rounds and strips and thrown into the hot soups just before serving.

EGG CUSTARD (for soups)
EIERSTICH

2 *eggs*	*mixed dried herbs*
2 *tablespoons of milk or stock*	*salt and pepper*
1 *teaspoon of potato flour (optional)*	

Beat the eggs together, then add the other ingredients. Pour into a well-greased tin or mould. Stand the tin in a baking pan of boiling water, cover with greased paper, and put into a moderate oven for about twenty minutes. Leave to cool and then cut into long thin strips, dice or cubes. Add to the soup as a garnish just before serving.

CLEAR SOUP
FLEISCHBRÜHE

1 *lb. stewing meat*	1 *parsnip*
½ *lb. bones*	1–2 *tomatoes*
1 *leek*	*salt and chopped mixed herbs*
2 *carrots*	1 *onion*

Put the meat, bones, salt, herbs and the vegetables, cleaned and chopped, into a pan of cold water and bring to the boil. Simmer for two or three hours. Strain first through a fine wire sieve, and then once more through a muslin cloth.

Clear soup is extremely popular in Germany, and is often garnished with tiny strips of pancakes (*Fridatten-suppe*), tiny dumplings, or egg custard, diced or cut into shapes. It also serves as a basis for semolina and sago soups.

CHICKEN NOODLE SOUP
HÜHNERBRÜHE MIT NUDELN

1 *boiling fowl*	*noodles, vermicelli type*
2 *carrots*	*dried herbs*
1 *leek*	*salt*
1 *parsnip*	

Joint the chicken, and with the liver, heart, neck and stomach put into a large pan with cold water. Add the vegetables and salt. Bring to the boil and skim. Simmer for two hours. Strain, and return the stock to the pan. Bring once more to the boil, add the noodles, a few dried herbs, and boil for a further fifteen minutes.

BEGGAR'S SOUP
BETTELMANNSUPPE

1 *lb. stewing steak cut into*
  pieces
1 *stick of celery*
1 *carrot*
1 *turnip*

1 *onion or leek*
½ *lb. potatoes*
1 *teaspoon of salt*
2 *pints of water*
salt and pepper

Prepare and chop all the vegetables and put with the other ingredients in a saucepan, and cover firmly. Cook very slowly for at least three hours. Season well.

Sprinkle with chopped parsley when serving.

QUEEN'S SOUP
KÖNIGINSUPPE

1 *lb. stewing lamb, or*
½ *a boiling chicken*
½ *lb. marrow bones*
1 *stick of celery*
1 *leek*
1 *parsnip*
2 *carrots*

1 *oz. butter*
1 *oz. flour*
½ *oz. chopped almonds*
1 *tablespoon sour cream*
1 *egg yolk*
salt, pepper and sugar

Boil the meat and vegetables with the bones and seasoning until the meat is tender. Strain and put aside the meat, keeping it warm. From the butter and flour make a brown roux. Add the stock and simmer gently for fifteen minutes. Beat the egg yolk and the cream together, add the almonds and quickly stir into the soup.

Strain once more, and re-heat. Cut the meat into small pieces, and just before serving add to the soup.

Small semolina dumplings are also served with this soup, or dumplings made from bone marrow. It is a popular restaurant soup.

GIBLET SOUP
GEFLÜGELKLEINSUPPE

Gizzard, feet, neck, wings, heart of a large bird	1 *tablespoon sour cream*
1 *large onion*	1 *tablespoon chopped parsley*
2 *leeks*	1 *oz. flour*
2 *carrots*	1 *oz. butter*
1 *lb. peeled potatoes*	*peppercorns*
	salt and pepper

Cut the neck into two or three pieces, and remove the windpipe and the gullet. Clean and wash the gizzard and pull off the thick inside membrane. Remove the skin and claws from the feet, and break the wings in halves. Wash the blood from the heart. Put the giblets into a pan of cold water, season well, and add all the vegetables except the potatoes. Cook for one and a half hours. Strain off the vegetables and giblets. Add the raw peeled potatoes to the stock, bring once more to the boil, and continue cooking until the potatoes are soft. Make a paste with the butter and flour and a little of the stock. Stir into the soup, pass through a sieve and re-heat.

Arrange the giblets in a soup tureen, stir the chopped parsley and the cream into the soup then pour it over the giblets.

GREEN PEA SOUP WITH SOUR CREAM
ERBSENSUPPE MIT SAURERSAHNE

1 *pint shelled peas*	1 *egg yolk*
1 *pint stock or water*	1 *tablespoon of chopped*
1 *oz. butter*	*parsley*
1 *oz. flour*	*salt, pepper and a pinch*
¼ *pint sour cream*	*of sugar*

Cook the peas in boiling stock or water until they are tender. Put aside to cool. Beat the egg with the butter and the flour, and pour into the cooled soup. Pass through a sieve and re-heat.

Mix the cream and parsley together and add to the soup. Serve with toasted squares of white bread or, in the South German fashion, with strips of smoked tongue.

To improve the flavour of this soup, a little Polish cooking sausage (*Grobe Mettwurst*) should be cooked with the peas.

DRIED BEAN SOUP
BOHNENSUPPE

6 *oz. dried white beans*	1 *oz. fat*
1 *stick of celery*	1 *oz. flour*
1 *carrot*	1 *meat extract cube*
1 *onion*	*bacon trimmings*
1 *parsnip*	*salt and pepper*

Soak the beans overnight. Cook the carrot, celery, parsnip and bacon trimmings in about three pints of water until you have a stock. Strain, and cook the beans in this liquid until they are tender. Slice the onion and fry lightly in fat. Add the flour and brown. Take four tablespoons of the beans and rub through a sieve. Mix with the onion, and return to the stock. For extra flavour dissolve a meat extract cube and stir into the soup. Season with salt and pepper, bring once more to the boil and serve hot. Germans frequently add meat extract to their soups and stews.

LENTIL SOUP WITH SAUSAGE
LINSENSUPPE MIT METTWURST

6 *oz. lentils*	1 *small Mettwurst*
3 *pints stock*	2 *oz. butter*
1 *onion*	1 *oz. flour*
1 *stick celery*	*salt and pepper*
2 *carrots*	

Soak the lentils overnight. Melt the butter in a pan, add the well-drained lentils and the cleaned and chopped vegetables. Cover the saucepan tightly and over a low heat simmer for about fifteen minutes. Add the stock, Mettwurst, salt and pepper, and cook gently for two hours. Take out the Mettwurst, pass the soup through a sieve, and return to the pan. The Mettwurst must be sliced before being returned to the soup. Re-heat, and thicken with the flour (mixed with a little milk or stock) and cook for a further five minutes. Serve with croûtons.

Mettwurst is known in England as Polish cooking sausage or coarse tea sausage. The sausage needed for this soup should be about four inches long.

SPRING SOUP
FRÜHLINGSSUPPE

2 *young carrots*
½ *a cauliflower*
a handful of young French beans

1 *lb. young peas, in their pods*
a little asparagus
4 *tablespoons shelled peas*
2 *pints seasoned meat stock*

As the carrots take the longest time to cook begin with them, scraped and sliced. Cook them in the stock until they are beginning to soften, then add the beans, broken into halves, the young pea pods and the shelled peas. The asparagus, peeled and chopped, and the cauliflower are added last of all. Do not let any of the vegetables mush.

Serve tiny meat dumplings, and an egg and lemon sauce with this soup.

As a variation omit the dumplings and add instead shrimps or prawns.

SEMOLINA DUMPLING SOUP
GRIESSNOCKERLSUPPE

2 *oz. semolina*
1 *oz. butter*
2 *pints meat stock*

1 *egg*
salt and pepper

Cream the egg and butter and stir into the hot stock. Bring to the boil, season, and throw in the semolina. Cook gently for one hour. Make some small dumplings and add them to the soup ten minutes before it is ready.

Any type of dumpling is suitable for this soup.

POTATO SOUP
ERDAPFELSUPPE NACH BÖHMISCHER ART
A Bohemian recipe

1 *lb. potatoes*
1 *oz. fat*
1 *oz. flour*
4 *oz. sliced Mettwurst*

dried mixed herbs
3 *pints vegetable stock*
salt and pepper

Peel and slice the potatoes, and cook them in the stock until they are tender. Take from the pan, rub through a sieve, then return to the stock. Melt the fat, blend in the flour to make a roux, adding a little milk to thin it. Stir this into the soup. Season, bring once more to the boil, and serve very hot with small pieces of Mettwurst floating on the top. Croûtons may also be added. The herbs are sprinkled on to the soup when it is in the plates.

TOMATO SOUP
TOMATENSUPPE

½ *lb. tomatoes*
3 *oz. bacon ends*
½ *oz. butter*
1 *medium chopped onion*

½ *pint meat stock*
1 *oz. flour*
mixed dried herbs

Melt the butter, and fry the bacon and chopped onion together. Add the tomatoes, chopped very small, then the stock. Cook until it is possible to rub the tomatoes through a sieve. Thicken with a paste of flour and stock, and cook for two minutes more. Season to taste and sprinkle with herbs.

PEASANT SOUP
BAUERNSUPPE

1 *large onion*
1 *lb. mixed root vegetables*
2 *tomatoes*
2 *oz. elbow macaroni*
½ *oz. mixed herbs*

1 *oz. bacon trimmings*
1 *oz. parmesan cheese*
2 *pints stock*
salt and pepper

Clean and prepare the vegetables, chopping them into small pieces. Sprinkle with salt. Fry the onion and bacon trimmings in a saucepan, add the vegetables, sauté for a moment, then pour in the hot stock. Cook until the vegetables are soft. About twenty minutes before the soup is ready throw in the macaroni.

Sprinkle the cheese over the soup when it is served.

ASPARAGUS SOUP
SPARGELSUPPE

1 *lb. asparagus*
1 *oz. flour*
1 *oz. butter*

sugar to taste
2 *pints seasoned stock*

Wash and peel the asparagus and cut into small pieces reserving the tips. Bring the stock to the boil, add the asparagus, slightly sweeten and cook until tender. Rub through a sieve. Cook the asparagus tips in boiling salted water until tender. Re-heat the sieved asparagus and thicken with a white paste made from the flour and butter with a little milk, then add the tips. An egg beaten into the soup just before serving is an improvement.

ONION SOUP
ZWIEBELSUPPE

1 *large chopped onion*
3 *tablespoons flour*
1½ *oz. butter*
1 *egg*

2 *tablespoons cream*
¾ *pint white stock or*
  milk
salt and pepper

Melt the butter, brown the onion, then add the flour. Pour in the stock or milk, season, and simmer gently for thirty minutes. Beat the egg with the cream, and stir into the soup just before serving.

Garnish with croûtons.

MUSHROOM SOUP
CHAMPIGNONSUPPE

1 *lb. mushrooms*
1 *oz. flour*
2 *oz. butter*

4 *egg yolks or 2 whole eggs*
croûtons
2 *pints stock*

Brown half of the butter with the flour. Gradually stir in the stock. Clean the mushrooms—use the button type if available, otherwise the large variety—and slice. Sauté in the remaining butter, and then add to the thickened stock. Cook gently until the mushrooms are tender.

Beat the eggs well, and loosen with either a little white wine or water, and pour over the croûtons. Throw these into the soup while it is still hot, leave for a moment and then serve immediately.

CAULIFLOWER SOUP
BLUMENKOHLSUPPE

1 *small cauliflower*   1 *oz. flour*
2 *pints water*   3 *tablespoons white wine*
1 *oz. butter*   *salt and pepper*
2 *egg yolks*

Instead of a whole small cauliflower, the stump of a large one will do, or left-over cauliflower.

From the cauliflower and water make a good foundation stock. Rub through a sieve, season well and return to the saucepan. Make a paste from the flour, butter and a little stock and thicken the soup. Beat the egg yolks together with the wine and pour in just before serving.

Serve with croûtons, very crisply fried.

CARROT SOUP
MOHRRÜBENSUPPE

½ *lb. carrots*   ½ *oz. butter*
2 *oz. soft breadcrumbs*   1 *sprig parsley*
1 *oz. bacon trimmings*   *sugar to taste*
1 *chopped onion*   *salt and pepper*
2 *pints meat stock*   *sour cream* (*optional*)

Wash, scrape and chop the carrots. Melt the butter in a saucepan and brown the breadcrumbs. Add the carrots, chopped onion, bacon, sugar, seasoning and parsley. Pour in the stock and cook until the carrots are soft. Rub through a sieve. When serving put one dessertspoon of sour cream into each plate of soup.

PUMPKIN SOUP
KÜRBISSUPPE

1 *lb. pumpkin*
lemon rind
4 *cloves*
cinnamon stick

1 *oz. butter*
1 *oz. flour*
1 *tablespoon wine vinegar*
sugar, salt and pepper

Peel and cut the pumpkin. Cook with the lemon rind, cloves, and cinnamon in two pints of water until tender. Remove the cinnamon (it can be used again) the cloves and the rind, and rub the pumpkin through a sieve. Brown the flour in butter, stir in the pumpkin, season and sweeten to taste, flavour with vinegar and serve.

White wine is better than vinegar if available.

SMELT AND WHITING SOUP
STINT-MERLANSUPPE

½ *lb. smelts*
½ *lb. whiting*
2 *pints fish stock or water*
1 *chopped onion*

1 *oz. butter*
1 *oz. flour*
2 *egg yolks*
juice of one lemon

Clean and trim the fish, cut into small pieces and fry in butter. Cover with chopped onion and dredge with flour. Fry a few moments longer, then add the stock or water. Season well, and cook gently for one hour. Pass through a sieve, and re-heat. Beat the egg yolks with the lemon juice, and pour into the soup.

OYSTER SOUP
AUSTERNSUPPE

1 *dozen oysters*
1 *small tin filleted anchovies*
1 *pint fish stock*
1 *oz. flour*
1 *oz. butter*

¼ *pint white wine*
1 *lemon*
1–2 *eggs*
salt and pepper

Open the oysters, remove their beards, and strain their liquid into a saucepan through a muslin cloth. Add the wine and the stock to the oyster liquid, season and bring to the boil. Throw in the shelled oysters for a few minutes, then quickly strain off, and put aside. Melt the butter and add the flour and a little stock to make a paste. Thicken the soup, and stir for two minutes. Add the anchovies, the eggs, well beaten, and the lemon juice. Immediately before serving throw back the oysters but do not let them cook.

If eggs are not available, then also omit the lemon juice, adding instead about half a pint of cream or the top of the milk.

HAMBURGER FRUIT SOUP
OBSTSUPPE NACH HAMBURGER ART

½ *lb. raspberries*
½ *lb. strawberries*
½ *lb. red currants*
½ *lb. sweet cherries*
½ *lb. Morello cherries*

½ *lb. bilberries*
1 *dessertspoon cornflour*
sweet biscuits
sugar to taste

Stone the cherries. Take a few of the strawberries, raspberries and sweet cherries and place them at the bottom of a soup tureen. Cook the remaining fruit together with water and sugar until soft. Thicken with cornflour, stir, and then pour over the fresh fruit.

Serve with the sweet biscuits.

EEL SOUP
AALSUPPE

¾ *lb. eel*
2 *pints meat stock*
1 *lb. pears, steamed in red wine*
3 *tablespoons tinned peas*
3 *shallots*

3 *bayleaves*
2 *tablespoons white wine*
6–8 *semolina dumplings*
flour
mixed dried herbs

Skin, bone and chop the eel into small pieces. Rub with salt and leave standing for one hour. Stew in salted water with the white wine, herbs and bayleaves until tender. Bring the stock with the shallots and the peas to the boil. Strain off the eel, and arrange in the bottom of a soup tureen together with the pears.

Pour the liquid from the eel into the boiling stock, and strain. Return the strained stock to the saucepan, throw in the dumplings, and cook for ten minutes. Thicken the soup with flour, and pour it over the eel and pears.

FISH SOUP
FISCHSUPPE

2 *lb. fish trimmings*
1 *chopped onion*
butter
sour cream

1 *oz. flour*
1 *egg yolk*
bayleaves and peppercorns
salt

Wash and dry the fish, then lightly fry in butter. Add the chopped onion, bay leaves, salt, and peppercorns. Fry for a few moments, then pour in about two pints of water. Bring to the boil, and cook gently for forty-five minutes. Strain, and return to the pan.

Melt more butter, add the flour, cook for two or three minutes, then stir in the fish stock. Bring once more to the boil.

Beat the egg yolk and cream together, and quickly add to the soup before serving.

Serve with croûtons.

A little white wine and mixed dried herbs may be added for additional flavour.

To make a brown fish soup, brown the flour in butter before adding the stock, and pour in half a glass of red wine just before serving.

APPLE BREAD SOUP

APFELBROTSUPPE

2 *lb. cooking apples*
grated rind of one lemon
   and its juice
a pinch of cinnamon

2 *oz. currants*
3 *oz. brown bread*
sugar to taste

Soak the bread and squeeze dry. Peel, core and slice the apples and cook with the bread in plenty of water until the apples are very soft. Rub through a strainer. Return to the saucepan, re-heat adding sugar, cinnamon and currants. Cook a few minutes until the currants have swollen. Add the lemon rind and juice. Bring once more to the boil. Small macaroon biscuits are often served with this type of soup.

POTATO SOUP
KARTOFFELSUPPE

2 *lb. raw peeled potatoes*
1 *stick of celery*
2 *carrots*
1 *leek*
1 *parsnip*
2 *cubes meat extract*

½ *oz. flour*
½ *oz. butter*
mixed dried herbs
salt and pepper
1 *tablespoon chopped parsley*

Put the potatoes into a pan of cold water and bring to the boil. Strain off the water and throw away. Pour another one and a half pints of water over the potatoes, add the vegetables, herbs, salt and pepper, and cook for one hour. Brown the flour and butter together in a saucepan until the mixture bubbles. Remove the carrots, leek, parsnip and celery from the soup—these are no longer needed. Rub the potatoes through a sieve, return to the pan and thicken with the butter and flour. Add the meat extract. Cook for another ten minutes. Sprinkle in the parsley just before serving.

COLD BEER SOUP
BIERKALTSCHALE

Very much a German and Austrian speciality. It is an acquired taste.

To one pint of light beer, add a handful of currants —which have previously been allowed to swell in a warm oven—about four ounces of brown breadcrumbs, one teaspoon of lemon juice and just a little ground cinnamon. Leave for fifteen minutes and serve quite cold.

ROSEHIP SOUP

HAGEBUTTENSUPPE

4 oz. dried rosehips
3 cloves
cinnamon stick
lemon rind

1 tablespoon white wine
1 oz. flour
1 oz. fat

Soak the rosehips until they are smooth. Boil in a pint of water with the rind, cinnamon and cloves until they are soft, then rub through a fine wire sieve. Brown the flour in the fat, and gradually add the soup. Sweeten to taste, add the wine, and serve hot.

BREAD SOUP

BROTSUPPE

5 oz. stale black bread
   (or rye)
1½ pints stock
1 oz. currants
1 oz. butter
1 teaspoon sugar

cinnamon stick
2 crushed cloves
chopped parsley
salt and pepper
lemon rind

Cut the bread into small squares and put into a saucepan. Pour over half a pint of tepid stock and leave the bread to soak. Add the rind, cinnamon, cloves, sugar, seasoning and the remainder of the stock. Cook for fifteen minutes then rub through a sieve, first removing the cinnamon stick.

Return the soup to the pan, stir in the butter and the currants, and simmer until the currants are swollen.

Serve hot, sprinkled with chopped parsley.

Other variations are to stir in an egg and lemon juice, or garnish with sliced frankfurter sausage, or chopped and sliced hard-boiled eggs.

MILK AND ALMOND SOUP

MANDELMILCHSUPPE

1 *oz. almonds*   1 *egg*
¾ *pint of milk*   *salt*

Blanch and grind the almonds, and leave to stand in cold milk for three-quarters of an hour. Add salt, rub through a sieve. Beat the yolk and the white of the egg separately. Stir the yolk into the milk. Just before serving fold in the egg white.

BEER OR WINE SOUP

BIER ODER WEINSUPPE

1 *pint light beer or white*   1 *teaspoon lemon flavoured*
  wine   *sugar*
1 *crushed clove*   1 *teaspoon cornflour*
a small piece of cinnamon   2 *eggs*
  stick

Bring the beer or wine, with the clove, cinnamon and sugar to the boil. Mix the cornflour with one tablespoon of liquid, and pour into the soup to thicken. Beat the egg yolks until they are frothy and stir into the soup.

Beat the egg whites stiffly, and drop dessertspoonfuls into boiling water. Lightly poach and serve floating on the top of the soup.

ELDERBERRY SOUP

HOLUNDERSUPPE

½ *lb. ripe elderberries*   *juice and rind of one lemon*
½ *lb. apples*   *sugar and salt*

Pull the elderberries from their stalks with a fork, and
cook in half a pint of water until soft. Rub through a
sieve. Thin the purée with about three-quarters of a
pint of boiling water. Add the apples, peeled and sliced,
and sweeten to taste. Add a little salt, and the lemon
rind, and continue cooking until the apples are soft.
Just before the soup is ready remove the rind, stir in the
lemon juice and, if needed, a little more sugar.

This soup is also prepared without apples, and the
rind and juice of an orange is sometimes used instead of
lemon.

Serve with small semolina dumplings.

FISH
FISCHE

FISH STOCK
FISCHBRÜHE

FOR FRESH WATER FISH

4 *pints water*	*parsley, thyme, bayleaves*
1 *glass white wine*	*salt and peppercorns*
2 *sliced onions*	

Cook all ingredients together for thirty or forty minutes. Strain before using.

GENERAL PURPOSE FISH STOCK

4 *pints water*	*peppercorns and a bayleaf*
1 *leek or onion*	1 *oz. butter*
2 *carrots*	1 *heaped teaspoon salt*

Bring to the boil and cook for ten minutes before adding the fish.

STEAMED FISH WITH MUSTARD SAUCE
FISCH GEDÄMPFT MIT SENF-SAUCE

Any white fish may be used for this dish. Trim and wash the fish, and place in a well-greased deep plate. Sprinkle it lightly with salt and pepper and a little lemon juice, and cover with greased paper. Place the plate over a pan of boiling water, cover with another plate, and steam for about thirty minutes. Turn the fish once during the cooking. (Sauce on next page.)

MUSTARD SAUCE

SENF-SAUCE

2 *tablespoons German mustard*   *fish stock or water*
3 *tablespoons of fat*   *salt and pepper*
4 *tablespoons of flour*

Melt the fat and add the flour. Cook for three minutes.
Thin with the stock or water, add the mustard, salt and
pepper, and pour over the fish while both are still hot.

EEL STEAMED IN BEER

AAL IN BIER

1½ *lb. eel*   1 *oz. flour*
1 *pint light beer*   *salt and pepper*
1 *chopped onion*   *chopped parsley*
1 *oz. butter*

Wash and skin the eel, and cut into inch-long pieces.
Bring the beer—to which has been added the onion and
seasoning—to the boil, before adding the eel. Steam
until the eel is tender. Strain off the liquid, and thicken
with a flour and water paste.

Arrange the pieces of eel in a deep dish, pour the
thickened beer stock over it, and serve with melted
butter and chopped parsley.

BLUE EEL

BLAU AAL

Cooking fish to give it a blue shimmer is a German
speciality. The general principle is not to scale the fish,

or to rub the outside with salt. Boiling tarragon or
wine vinegar is poured over the fish, and it is left to
stand in a draught for ten minutes.

Trout, pike, eel, herrings and mackerel are favourite
fish for cooking in this manner.

2 *lb. eel*	1 *leek*
¼ *pint boiling vinegar*	*chopped thyme, sage, parsley*
1 *piece celery*	*salt and pepper*
2 *carrots*	*fish stock*

Wash but do not skin the eel, and rub it well with
salt (eel is an exception to the general rule). Pour over
it the boiling vinegar and leave standing in a draught
for ten or fifteen minutes. Cut into small pieces and
cook with the other ingredients until it is tender, about
an hour.

Strain and serve with melted butter, parsley and
slices of lemon.

FISH RAGOUT

FISCHRAGOUT

1 *lb. cooked boned white fish*	1 *oz. breadcrumbs*
½ *lb. mushrooms*	½ *oz. butter*
	Béchamel sauce

Cut the fish into small pieces, roll in the sauce and
arrange in a fireproof casserole. Slice the mushrooms
and toss in melted butter. Cover the fish with mushrooms, sprinkle with brown breadcrumbs and dot with
butter. Season and bake in the oven until the fish is
heated through and the mushrooms cooked.

Serve with Béchamel sauce (see page 151).

BLUE TROUT

BLAUE FORELLE

The trout should be cooked as soon as it is caught; quickly cleaned and placed in a pan of boiling fish stock.

Take the pan from the fire and leave the trout in it for five minutes.

Serve quite plainly with boiled potatoes which have been tossed in butter and sprinkled with chopped parsley.

Use No. 1 fish stock (see page 30) for fresh water fish.

FISH FRICASSEE

FISCHFRIKASSEE

1½ *lb. cooked, boned white fish*	¼ *pint cider*
	juice of half a lemon
3 *oz. steamed mushrooms*	2 *egg yolks beaten*
1 *oz. flour*	*salt and pepper*
1 *oz. chopped onion*	*capers*
¾ *pint fish stock*	1 *oz. butter*

Brown the butter with the flour, add the chopped onion and fry for three minutes. Stir in the stock and the cider and cook gently until the onion is tender. Pour through a sieve. Add the egg yolks, lemon juice, salt and pepper. Return three-quarters of this sauce to the pan, add the cooked fish, and simmer until the fish is re-heated.

Arrange pyramid shape on a serving dish, garnish with capers and pour over the rest of the sauce, which should be hot. If available, add shrimps both for their flavour and decorative value.

COLD SALMON
WITH REMOULADE SAUCE

KALTER LACHS MIT REMOULADEN SAUCE

2 lb. cold cooked salmon
1 cup mayonnaise
¼ teaspoon anchovy essence
1 teaspoon German mustard
1 teaspoon chopped chervil

grated lemon rind
parsley
1 tablespoon chopped gherkins
1 tablespoon capers

In a cool bowl mix the mayonnaise, gherkins and capers and leave for one hour. Rub through a fine wire sieve. Add the chopped parsley, chervil, mustard and anchovy essence and lemon rind.

Serve this sauce in a sauce-boat.

Arrange the salmon on a wooden platter, garnished with slices of lemon and sprigs of parsley.

Accompany with a cucumber salad.

BLUE SALMON

BLAU LACHS

2 lb. fresh salmon
½ bottle white wine
4 oz. butter
3 bayleaves

tarragon vinegar (boiling)
salt and peppercorns
mixed dried herbs
parsley and lemon

Trim the fish and place in a large pan or fish kettle. Pour over the boiling vinegar and leave standing in a draught for ten minutes. Add the wine, salt, peppercorns, herbs, bay leaves and butter and bring once to the boil. Reduce the heat, and simmer gently ior one hour.

Take the fish carefully from the pan, arrange on a warm dish, and serve with a Hollandaise or shrimp sauce—or sour cream mixed with horse radish.

Dress with sliced lemon and sprigs of fresh parsley.

GREEN EEL WITH CUCUMBER SALAD
GRÜNER AAL MIT GURKENSALAT

2 *lb. eel*
1 *tablespoon mixed dried*
  herbs
parsley
seasoning
3 *bay leaves*

1 *cup sour cream*
juice of half a lemon
cucumber
1 *oz. flour*
1 *oz. butter*

Skin and bone the eel and cut into pieces two inches long. Put into boiling water together with the seasonings, herbs, and lemon juice. Cook slowly until the eel is tender. Strain off the eel and pour the stock through a sieve.

Make a brown roux with the flour and butter, and add a little of the stock to thin it. Thicken the remainder of the stock with the roux, stirring all the time. Return the eel to the stock, add the cream and cook for a further five minutes. Serve with a cucumber salad and garnished with sprigs of parsley.

Do not use too much water when cooking the eel, as it is not meant to swim in the sauce when served.

BAKED SKATE WITH SAUERKRAUT
ROCHEN MIT SAUERKRAUT

1 *lb. skate*	1 *small sliced onion*
2 *tablespoons butter*	*bayleaves, peppercorns, cloves*
flour	½ *pint milk*
salt	

Cut the fish into steaks, rub with salt and leave for one hour.

Bring the milk with the onion, cloves, bay leaves and peppercorns to the boil, then add the fish. Let the milk boil once more and leave the fish to simmer for only five minutes—no longer.

Strain from the liquid and leave to dry on a sieve. Rub with melted butter or warm olive oil, and roll in seasoned flour. Wrap in cooking paper, bake in hot oven. Serve with boiled sauerkraut and a tomato salad.

BOILED SKATE WITH ONION BUTTER
ROCHEN GEKÖCHT MIT ZWIEBELBUTTER

2 *lb. skate*	*peppercorns*
2 *large chopped onions*	*bayleaves and mixed dried*
2 *oz. butter*	*herbs*
1 *tablespoon chopped parsley*	*juice of half a lemon*
truffle (optional)	3 *cloves*

Wash and trim the fish, rub in salt and lemon and leave for one hour. Well cover with water and stew for thirty minutes with the peppercorns, bayleaves, cloves and herbs.

Cool, then carefully skin the fish. Re-heat.

Melt the butter, brown the onions, add a little lemon juice, chopped parsley and the truffle, stir, and pour over the fish just before serving.

The stock in which the skate has been cooked could be utilised next day for a fish soup.

FISH WITH WHITE CABBAGE AND CARRAWAY SEEDS

FISCHE MIT KÜMMELKRAUT

1 *lb. cod*	*carraway seeds*
1 *lb. potatoes*	*salt*
1 *shredded white cabbage*	2 *oz. butter*

Melt the butter in a saucepan, add the cabbage, potatoes, peeled and sliced, the salt and carraway seeds and about half a cup of boiling water. Bring slowly to the boil, lower the heat and cook gently for thirty minutes.

Cut the fish into about three pieces and put on top of the cabbage. Cook covered for a further ten or fifteen minutes. Leave in the pan for ten more minutes after cooking, over the smallest possible heat. Serve with slices of lemon.

BLUE CARP

BLAU KARPFEN

Carp is the north German traditional Christmas Eve dish, and on this occasion it is often cooked 'blue'. Also, at this time it is the custom not to scale the fish, whatever method is used, so that everyone eating the carp can save one scale, which he must put into his purse as a charm to bring him luck the whole year through.

Choose a large carp and tie its tail and snout together to form a circle. Place in a large pan and pour boiling wine vinegar over it. Leave the fish in a draught for ten minutes. Bring to the boil in the same pan with some sliced onions, peppercorns, salt and mixed dried herbs. Stand the pan on the side of the stove with a little heat and leave until the carp is tender.

Rinse the fish quickly, first in hot water, then in cold. Return to the stock just long enough to re-heat.

Strain and serve with a sauce made from cream and horse radish. In Hamburg they add a dessertspoon of whipped cream on top of the fish when serving, while in the south they like to serve a few capers with the sauce. In Silesia, separate bowls containing chopped parsley, and browned butter seem to be the rule.

CARP COOKED IN BEER

KARPFEN IN BIER

2 *lb. carp*	½ *oz. flour*
1 *oz. butter*	1 *pint beer*
3 *tablespoons chopped carrot and leek*	*lemon juice and rind*
	2 *oz. gingerbread cut in cubes*
1 *large onion*	*salt and sugar*

Cut the carp into steaks and lay in either lemon juice or wine vinegar for thirty minutes.

Brown the butter and the flour, add the onion and the chopped vegetables. Simmer. Pour some of the beer over the gingerbread and when it is soft add to the vegetables. Pour in the rest of the beer, the lemon juice and rind, and season. Stir the sauce well, and lay the fish in it. Continue cooking over the lowest possible heat until the fish is tender.

Strain, and serve with raspberry juice or jelly, and sprinkle with salt and sugar.

COOKING COD IN GERMANY

Apart from the usual boiling or steaming of cod, the Germans are fond of serving it lightly poached in white wine, with thickly sliced onions and flavoured with garlic. Thin slices of hard-boiled egg are added as a garnish, or young French beans, and croûtons.

Cheap cuts of cod are floured or dipped in egg and breadcrumbs, fried and laid on a 'bed' of creamed spinach over which melted butter is poured.

Mushrooms are extensively used with fish, especially the button type which are creamed and poured over the fish just before serving.

COD HAMBURGER STYLE

KABELJAU NACH HAMBURGER ART

2 *lb. cod*
½ *pint white wine*
juice of one lemon
1 *oz. soft breadcrumbs*

1 *doz. tinned oysters*
1 *oz. butter*
salt, peppercorns and mace

Clean the fish, rub with salt and lemon juice. Leave in a cool place for two hours. Put in a pan with an equal quantity of white wine and water, add peppercorns and mace, and cook until tender.

Strain off the fish, and pour the liquid through a sieve.

Melt the butter, fry the breadcrumbs and gradually pour in the liquid. Add the oysters, bring the sauce once to the boil, then quickly take from the heat.

Arrange the fish on a platter, pour over it the oyster sauce, and garnish with slices of lemon.

BAKED COD WITH MUSHROOMS
GEBRATENER KABELJAU MIT PILZEN

2 *lb. cod*	$\frac{1}{4}$ *lb. mushrooms*
1 *stick celery*	*juice of one lemon*
1 *leek*	*salt, peppercorns and bayleaves*
1 *parsnip*	$\frac{1}{4}$ *pint white wine*

Clean the fish, add peppercorns and bayleaves, rub it with salt and lemon juice and leave for thirty minutes. Place it in a greased earthenware casserole and surround it with thinly sliced vegetables. Pour over the wine, dot with butter and bake in a hot oven for thirty minutes, basting frequently.

Serve the fish on a warmed dish garnished with the vegetables.

SOUSED HERRINGS
BRATHERINGE, EINGELEGT

Cut off the heads and tails of as many herrings as required. Clean them, reserving the roes. Roll the herrings in flour, and fry in hot oil or other fat, browning both sides. Fry the roes separately. Leave to cool.

Bring two-thirds vinegar, to one-third water, with a

little olive oil, to the boil. Add a few peppercorns, mustard seed, bayleaves and some sliced onion. Leave to become quite cold.

Lay the cooled herrings in a flat dish, and pour over them the marinade. Leave for twenty-four hours. The roes are usually laid on top.

FRESH HADDOCK HAMBURG STYLE
SCHELLFISCH NACH HAMBURGER ART

2 *lb. haddock*	¼ *pint sour cream*
1 *lb. potatoes*	2 *beaten eggs*
1 *small chopped onion*	*butter*

Remove the head from the fish: clean and cut into small pieces. Salt and leave for one hour. Peel and slice the potatoes, then arrange in alternate layers with the fish in a buttered casserole. Brown the onion in butter, add to the casserole, and sprinkle with pepper. Beat the eggs and cream together, pour over the fish, and bake for a good thirty minutes in a moderate oven.

HERRINGS AND ONIONS
FRISCHE HERINGE MIT ZWIEBELN

2 *lb. herrings*	½ *pint wine vinegar*
4 *large sliced onions*	1 *oz. butter*

Clean the herrings, remove heads and tails, and rub the insides only with salt. Leave for half an hour.

Lightly fry the onions in butter, then lay the herrings

on top of them. Pour over the vinegar, and slowly cook the fish and onions together until tender.

The herrings should have a blue shimmer when cooked.

BISMARCK HERRING
BISMARCKHERINGE

2 *lb. herrings*	*salt and cayenne pepper*
slices of onion	*vinegar*

Scale and clean the herrings and leave to soak overnight in vinegar. Next day, remove the heads and tails and the centre bone. Divide the herrings lengthways. Arrange a layer of herring fillets at the bottom of a dish, sprinkle with salt and pepper and a few slices of onion. Add another layer of fillets, sprinkle with salt and pepper, and add the sliced onion. Repeat until all the herrings are used up.

Leave for twenty-four hours, by which time they will be ready for eating.

BAKED HERRINGS
HERINGS-AUFLAUF

4 *salted herrings*	½ *pint sour cream*
2 *lb. raw peeled potatoes*	*butter*
3 *sliced onions*	*breadcrumbs*
2 *egg yolks*	

Cook the potatoes in salted water, drain and slice. Bone and chop the herrings, and mix with the onions.

At the bottom of a casserole arrange a layer of potatoes, then one of fish and onions. Repeat until all the ingredients are used up. The top layer must be of potatoes.

Beat the yolks and the cream together and pour over the potatoes. Sprinkle with breadcrumbs and dot with butter.

Bake in a moderate oven for about three-quarters of an hour.

COLLARED HERRINGS

ROLLMOPS

2 *lb. fresh herrings*	*chopped sour gherkins*
tarragon vinegar	*chopped onion*
milk	*mustard seed*
peppercorns, bayleaves	

Clean the herrings, removing heads and tails, and soak in water for twelve hours, then in milk for another twelve hours.

Split them carefully down the centre, and bone. Into each herring fillet put some orion, gherkin and peppercorns. Roll them up and fix with a small stick.

When they are all ready, lay them in a large jar. Beat the herring roes until they are smooth and mix with enough vinegar—previously boiled with onions and cooled—to fill the jar. In between the rolled herrings put some bayleaves, mustard seed, peppercorns, slices of onion and pieces of gherkin.

Leave three or four days.

Serve, without the marinade, either as they are or with sour cream poured over them.

MACKEREL WITH BACON
MAKRELEN MIT SPECK

2 *mackerel*   *tomatoes as a garnish*
4 *large rashers of bacon* *butter for greasing baking dish*
salt and pepper

Thoroughly clean the fish and carefully bone, removing the head and tail. Divide into fillets and rub well with salt and pepper. Place a fillet on each slice of bacon. Roll and fix with a cocktail stick or tie with cotton.

Wash and skin as many tomatoes as you will require to cover the bottom of a baking dish. Cut the tomatoes into thick slices and arrange these at the bottom of a well greased baking dish. Place the bacon rolls on top of the tomatoes, sprinkle with pepper and salt, cover the dish and bake in a moderate oven for about 20 minutes. Uncover and bake for another five minutes but do not allow the bacon to become crisp.

MACKEREL
WITH RED CURRANT SAUCE
MAKRELEN MIT JOHANNISBEERENSAUCE

1 *mackerel*   *red currant jelly*
tarragon or wine vinegar (boiling)

Clean the fish, rub the inside only with salt and pour over the boiling vinegar. Stand the fish in a draught for ten minutes.

Make three slits across the back and cook in a fish stock or boiling water for ten to fifteen minutes.

Serve with warmed red currant jelly or melted butter.

Hollandaise sauce is also a good accompaniment to mackerel cooked 'blue'.

FISH WITH CAULIFLOWER
FISCH MIT BLUMENKOHL

2 *lb. white fish*	*fish stock*
1 *large cauliflower*	*mixed dried herbs, bayleaves*
3 *oz. butter*	*salt and peppercorns*
1 *oz. flour*	*lemon*
1 *egg yolk*	

Clean the fish, rub in salt and lemon juice and leave for thirty minutes. Wash the cauliflower, and cook until tender, but not broken. Strain, and leave on the side of the stove to keep warm.

Bring the fish stock to the boil with the peppercorns, bayleaves and herbs, add the fish and cook until tender. Take out the fish and remove all skin and bones.

Arrange the fish in a serving dish, surrounded by the cauliflower, divided into tiny clumps.

Make a brown roux with the butter and flour, thin with fish stock, season with salt and pepper, add a few drops of lemon juice and bind with the egg yolk. Stir well, and pour over the fish and cauliflower.

BAKED FISH WITH SAUERKRAUT
FISCH MIT SAUERKRAUT

2 *lb. fish*	1 *oz. butter*
1 *lb. cooked sauerkraut*	*salt and pepper*
$\frac{1}{4}$ *pint milk*	

Arrange the cleaned and prepared fish with the sauer-kraut in a greased casserole. Bring the milk and butter to the boil and pour over the fish. Season with salt and pepper, and bake in a hot oven for twenty minutes.

FISH COOKED GREEN
FISCH, GRÜN GEKOCHT

1 *lb. fish*	*salt and pepper*
2 *oz. butter*	*parsley and bayleaves*
2 *oz. flour*	*dill and thyme*
1 *small sliced onion*	*soft breadcrumbs*

Skin and bone the fish and cut into medium sized pieces. Put in a pan of boiling salted water, adding the bayleaves, dill, thyme and a small nob of butter. Bring once to the boil, then stand on the side of the stove almost to finish cooking in the boiling water, but without any direct heat.

Make a roux with the butter and flour, add the breadcrumbs and enough of the fish water to make a smooth but thick sauce. Simmer for about three minutes.

Strain the fish from the pan, and lay in the sauce. Leave over a very low heat until the fish is quite tender. Sprinkle with chopped parsley just before serving.

It simplifies things enormously if the sauce is made in a fireproof casserole which is nice enough to bring to the table, for the fish and sauce are served together.

FISH AND POTATO DISH

LABSKAUS

1 *lb. fish*	1 *bayleaf*
2 *lb. potatoes*	3 *onions*
½ *pint broth*	6 *peppercorns*
3 *oz. fat*	*salt*

Wash, peel and finely chop the onions. Cut the fish into small pieces and cook until tender. Peel the potatoes, cut them into quarters and cook long enough to coarsely mash them. Melt the fat—it is better when this has a good bacon flavour—and lightly fry the onions until they are a golden brown. Add the potatoes, the bayleaf, salt and peppercorns then, lastly, the strained fish. Fry all these ingredients together until they are very hot but not too much mixed up—you do not want a mash. Each ingredient should be identifiable.

This is a popular fisherman's recipe in Oldenburg, Schleswig Holstein. Sometimes instead of fish, salted pork, corned beef or another type of meat is used. The type of fish used depends on the catch and on individual taste. Salted cod or smoked haddock makes excellent *Labskaus.*

PIKE WITH CAULIFLOWER CHEESE

HECHT AUFLAUF

1 *pike*	*grated cheese*
1 *partly cooked cauliflower*	*lemon juice and rind*
1 *oz. butter*	*nutmeg*
breadcrumbs	*flour*

Butter a casserole and sprinkle with breadcrumbs. Clean the fish, and cut into small pieces. Arrange in the dish, and completely cover with the cauliflower.

Thicken the cauliflower water with flour, add the nutmeg and the juice and rind of the lemon, stir and simmer until it has a good flavour. Remove the rind, and pour the sauce over the cauliflower. Sprinkle liberally with grated cheese and breadcrumbs, dot with butter and bake in a hot oven for thirty minutes.

LOBSTER COOKED IN BEER
HUMMER IN WEISSBIER

1 *pint of light beer*	*carraway seeds*
1 *chicken lobster*	*pepper*
3 *shallots*	

Cook the lobster from twenty to forty minutes, according to the size. When it is tender, remove the flesh from the shell, and dice.

Bring the beer with the shallots, pepper and carraway seeds to the boil, thicken with a little flour, and strain.

Arrange the lobster on a plate and pour over it the beer sauce.

LARDED FISH WITH VEGETABLES
GESPICKTER FISCH MIT GEMÜSEN

2 *lb. cod or similar fish*	*juice of one lemon*
2 *oz. larding*	½ *lb. carrots*
4 *oz. butter*	½ *lb. string beans*
¼ *pint sour cream*	½ *lb. tomatoes*
1 *oz. flour*	*mixed herbs*

For this recipe a whole fish is the best, but if not available a large piece of a thick fish will do.

Clean and scale the fish, and rub with salt. Cut the larding into small lengths and lard one side of the fish only. Sprinkle with the lemon juice, and leave the fish for one hour.

Melt the butter in a baking tin, and lay the fish in it, larded side up. Put into a hot oven, and bake for forty minutes, basting frequently.

Cut the tomatoes into halves and bake in the oven at the same time as the fish. Cook the carrots and beans separately.

Take the fish from the pan, and lay, larded side uppermost, on a hot plate. Stir the flour into the fat, add the cream and cook on top of the stove until thick. A little white wine may be added if available. Season with salt and pepper, and flavour with the herbs.

Garnish the fish with the vegetables and serve the sauce in a sauceboat.

Some recipes say that it is better to skin the fish before larding. Although this takes more time and effort it makes a vast improvement.

Rice should be served with larded fish, as well as mushrooms or cauliflower.

HERRINGS AND POTATOES

HERINGSKARTOFFELN

2 *lb. potatoes*	2 *oz. flour*
3 *salted herrings*	*a little chopped onion*
2 *oz. butter*	½ *pint milk*

Cook the potatoes in their skins, cool, then peel and slice.

Skin and bone the herrings and cut into small pieces.

Brown the butter and flour, add the onion, and the milk, and stir. Add the herrings and simmer for ten minutes. When the herrings are done, add the potatoes and leave them in the pan just long enough to re-heat.

Serve, liberally sprinkled with chopped parsley.

EGG DISHES
EIERSPEISEN

PEASANT'S BREAKFAST
BAUERNFRUEHSTUECK

This is a really large meal usually consisting of scrambled eggs, slices of cooked meat, reheated, fried potatoes, bacon and tomatoes as well as mixed vegetables.

In some parts of the country it can also mean a plate of mixed garlic sausages.

SCRAMBLED EGGS WITH CHIVES
RUEHREI MIT SCHNITTLAUCH

4 eggs
finely chopped chives to taste
finely chopped fat bacon

salt and pepper
butter for frying

Beat the eggs, adding salt and pepper, until they are thoroughly broken but not smooth. Heat a frying pan, fry the pieces of bacon and enough butter to cook the eggs. Add the beaten eggs and the chopped chives, stir lightly and cook long enough to set the eggs.

Or you can prepare the scrambled eggs separately, then sprinkle the chopped chives and tiny pieces of fried bacon over them when serving.

BOILED EGG IN BREADCRUMBS
PANIERTE EIER

4 eggs
1 beaten egg white

1 oz. flour
breadcrumbs

Put the eggs into a pan with cold water, and as soon as the water comes to the boil take from the pan and shell as quickly as possible. Roll the eggs in flour, egg white and breadcrumbs to form a thick crust. Drop immediately into boiling fat.

Serve either hot or cold on a bed of cooked spinach, and pour over some Béchamel sauce (see page 151). Or serve cold on toast with mayonnaise sauce.

SOUFFLE OMELETTE

OMELETT

3 *egg yolks*	1 *tablespoon lemon juice*
3 *egg whites*	*a pinch of salt*
2 *oz. sugar*	

Beat the egg yolks and the sugar to a cream. Add the salt and lemon juice. Fold in the egg whites.

Melt a little butter in a pan, pour in the egg mixture, and cook gently for ten to fifteen minutes. With a spatula take it from the pan, fill with jam, preferably apricot, and fold over. Serve immediately.

PEASANT OMELETTE

BAUERNOMELETT

8 *eggs*	2 *oz. bacon*
3 *oz. butter*	1 *chopped onion*
6 *oz. cooked and diced potatoes*	*chopped parsley*

This amount makes three omelettes.

Dice and lightly fry the bacon. Add the potatoes, and the onion.

In another pan, melt some of the butter, and put into it about one-third of the bacon, onion and potatoes. Lightly beat the eggs with a little salt and chopped parsley. Pour one-third into the omelette pan and cook it over a quick fire until it sets.

EMPEROR'S PANCAKE

KAISERSCHMARREN

½ *pint milk*	1 *oz. raisins*
4 *oz. flour*	1 *oz. melted butter*
2 *egg yolks*	2 *beaten egg whites*
1 *oz. sugar*	*butter for frying*

Beat the flour and milk together, and gradually add the egg yolks. Continue beating for several minutes, then add the sugar, raisins, and the melted butter. Lastly, fold in the egg whites.

Melt a little more butter in an omelette pan, then pour in the batter. Brown on both sides, and put on to a hot plate. Sprinkle with sugar and pull to pieces with two forks before serving.

EGG STICKS

EIERSTANGEN

Mix some Béchamel sauce (see page 151) with chopped hard-boiled egg. Shape into small sticks, roll in bread-crumbs, and bake in the oven until a golden brown.

STUFFED EGGS
GEFÜLLTE EIER

Boil as many eggs as needed very hard, shell, cut in halves and scoop out the centres.

Fill with any of the following mixtures:

Pounded anchovies, salt and pepper, mixed with the mashed yolks.

Mashed yolks mixed with dry mustard, chopped capers and finely chopped parsley.

Chopped cold chicken, cooked chopped celery, and mayonnaise, mixed with the chopped yolks.

Meat salad (see page 139) and chopped yolks.

Cold fish, rubbed through a sieve, mixed with the mashed yolks and a little paprika, and garnished with chopped tomato.

Mashed yolks with crab, garnished with mayonnaise. Top each half with a shrimp.

POACHED EGGS
VERLORENE EIER

Bring some water with a little vinegar to the boil. Break an egg in a cup, stir the water quickly to make a well into which the egg must be gently slipped. Remove with a draining spoon and place on a slice of toast, spread with goose-liver butter.

POACHED EGGS IN TOMATO CUPS
VERLORENE EIER IN TOMATEN

Poach as many eggs as are required. Cut some tomatoes in half, and scoop out the centres. Into each half drop a poached egg, and pour over them some remoulade sauce (see page 155).

HARD BOILED EGGS
IN PIQUANT SAUCE
SAURE EIER

Melt some butter; add flour, and some diced fat bacon. Stir and fry for a few minutes. Thin with a little boiling water and wine, season with salt and pepper, sweeten to taste and cook the sauce until it is smooth.

Shell some hard-boiled eggs, and roll them in the hot sauce. Serve with boiled potatoes, tossed in butter and sprinkled with chopped parsley.

COLOURED EASTER EGGS
BUNTE EIER

Boil the eggs until they are hard. To colour them red, leave them in water to which cochineal has been added. Red cabbage water will turn them a vivid violet colour. Spinach water turns them green. Adding the brown outside leaves of an onion to the cooking water will turn the egg shells brown.

SOUFFLE PANCAKE
EIERKUCHEN

2 *egg yolks*
1 *pint milk*
1 *teaspoon baking powder*

½ *lb. flour*
2 *egg whites (beaten)*

Beat the yolks and milk together with a pinch of salt, then add to the flour and baking powder. Beat well to a smooth batter. Fold in the egg whites. Pour a quarter of the mixture into a pan with a little melted butter. Fry on one side, then turn quickly with a spatula and fry the other side. Spread with jam, fold over and serve at once.

Use the rest of the batter in the same way.

GOOSE

GANS

ROAST goose is the German traditional Christmas Day dish, and is almost invariably served with red cabbage. In some parts of Germany, Thüringen for example, they also serve potato dumplings made from raw potatoes, and in other districts noodles are usual as an accompaniment.

This recipe was given me by my old German cook, many years ago. She came from South Germany and was a true peasant type.

Stuff the inside of a dressed goose with apples, they may be peeled or not, but certainly cored. Sew up the goose and lay on the grid in a large roasting pan, breast down, and pour over it half a pint of boiling water. Add a chopped onion, and bake in a moderate oven for thirty to forty minutes. Remove the goose from the pan, take away the grid, and return the goose, this time breast up. Baste frequently with boiling water. From time to time prick the skin of the goose, about the throat and wings, to allow the fat to run. When the goose begins to change colour, start to baste with goose fat. When it has been roasting for two hours, skim off some of the fat. About fifteen minutes before it is ready, baste with a few tablespoons of cold water, so that the skin becomes crisp.

Take the goose from the pan, thicken the gravy, and pass it through a strainer.

GOOSE STUFFINGS
GÄNSE FÜLLUNGEN

1. Cook together in a little water some peeled and chopped apples, peeled chestnuts, a handful of stoned raisins, the liver and giblets of the goose, and one peeled and sliced potato. When the mixture is almost brown, stuff firmly into the goose.

2. Put into a thick bottomed pan two pounds of peeled and cored cooking apples, one pound of soaked and stoned prunes, five ounces of sugar, and just enough water to prevent burning. Cook slowly for about three hours until you have the consistency of a thick jam. The stuffing is then ready to use.

STUFFED GOOSE NECK
GEFÜLLTER GÄNSEHALS

1 *goose liver*	1 *dessertspoon truffle*
6 *oz. pork*	1 *chopped onion*
4 *oz. fat bacon*	*chopped parsley and marjoram*
2 *white rolls*	*madeira*
butter	

Soak the liver overnight in milk, and next day steam in butter until it is tender. Put the pork and bacon through a mincer, then fry in butter with the onion. Soak the bread, and squeeze dry. Put with the liver through the mincer.

Now mix all these ingredients together, flavour with herbs and the truffle, and moisten with madeira.

Carefully remove the fat, bones and muscle from the goose neck, and stuff the skin with the forcemeat until it looks rather like a fat sausage. Sew it firmly at both ends, and fry in butter until it is brown and crisp. Serve hot or cold, cut into thick slices.

This is considered a great delicacy in Germany and in the surrounding countries.

GOOSE GIBLETS
GÄNSEKLEIN

head, neck, heart, feet, stomach,	1 *onion*
wings, of a goose	1 *oz. flour*
1 *parsnip*	1 *oz. butter*
1 *leek*	1 *tablespoon of chopped*
2 *carrots*	*parsley*

Chop off the beak and take out the eyes from the head. Cut the neck into two, and break the wings from the bend of the bone. Clean the stomach (remove its thick skin both inside and out), and slice. Chop off the claws from the feet, then skin. Wash all these and together with all the vegetables (except the onion) cook until tender. Melt the butter, lightly fry the chopped onion, add the flour, and some of the giblet stock. Cook for two minutes, then add the parsley.

Take out the pieces of goose with a draining spoon, arrange on a hot plate and cover with the onion sauce. Surround with cooked rice or mashed potatoes.

In Saxony, they cook stewing steak with the giblets, and when the meat is almost tender, throw in some tiny dumplings. Instead of rice, they use cauliflower.

Like the stuffed goose neck, this dish is highly rated as a delicacy.

GOOSE LIVER PASTE
GÄNSELEBERBUTTER

1 *goose liver*   4 *oz. butter*
¼ *pint madeira*   1 *slice stale bread*
2 *tablespoons mixed dried*   *parmesan cheese*
  herbs   *salt and cayenne pepper*

Sauté the liver in about half an ounce of butter, and
when tender mash with a fork. Soak the bread in the
madeira, then squeeze it dry through a cloth, saving
the wine. Dampen the herbs with the madeira, cream
the remaining butter, then mix all the ingredients together—you only need the smallest amount of cheese.
Rub the paste through a fine sieve, then it is ready for
spreading on slices of rye bread.

GOOSE DRIPPING
GÄNSEFETT

Cut pieces of the skin and the fat of a goose into small
pieces, put into a thick-bottomed pan, and heat over a
fierce fire until the fat begins to melt. Reduce the heat
and leave the fat to melt for three hours. About half an
hour before it is ready, add an onion, peeled and
quartered, and one unpeeled cooking apple. (If the
apple should burst, take it out of the pan at once,
otherwise the fat will not be clear.) Cook on a fierce
heat for a moment to brown, then pour through a
muslin bag or a very fine wire sieve. Leave to set, but
while still warm spread on bread and sprinkle with salt.
Coarse brown bread is the best. Goose dripping is also

spread over potatoes which have been boiled, and served in their skins.

GOOSE LIVER
WITH APPLES AND ONIONS

GÄNSELEBER MIT ÄPFELN UND ZWIEBELN

1 *goose liver*
2 *peeled and sliced apples*
1 *large sliced onion*

butter
salt and paprika
breadcrumbs

Soak the liver in milk for one hour. Dry, and roll in salt, paprika and breadcrumbs. Lightly fry in butter. Add the sliced apples and onions, and fry until the liver is tender.

Some German cooks omit the breadcrumbs, and fry each ingredient separately, serving them together, however, on a hot plate with a sauce made from madeira and truffles.

ROAST CHICKEN

BRATHUHN

young chicken
butter
mixed herbs

salt and pepper
brandy or meat stock

Divide the chicken into four, rub with salt, and lay in a casserole with melted butter. Roast until tender, basting from time to time with a little brandy or meat stock. Take the wings and breast from the pan ten minutes before the legs.

Thicken the gravy with a little flour, season with salt and pepper, add a few mixed herbs and cook for five minutes.

Serve the sauce either separately or poured over the chicken.

Button mushrooms, lightly sautéed, may also be added to the sauce, or chopped parsley. White or red wine may be used instead of brandy. Or a gill of sour cream is sometimes mixed with the gravy, in which case the flour should be omitted.

YOUNG CHICKEN HUNTER'S STYLE

JUNGES HUHN NACH JÄGER ART

1 *young chicken*
2 *tablespoons olive oil*
1 *small glass brandy*
4 *oz. sliced mushrooms*

6 *shallots*
mixed dried herbs
1 *tablespoon of tomato purée*

Joint the chicken, and fry gently in oil until the outside is browned and the flesh cooked through.

Take from the pan, and keep hot while the sauce is being made.

Using the same pan, lightly fry the mushrooms and the shallots. Add the tomato purée and the herbs, stir, and pour in the brandy. Cook for two or three minutes, then pour over the chicken.

Serve with a green salad and boiled noodles, over which some poppy seeds have been sprinkled.

PULLETS PEASANT STYLE
MASTHUHN NACH BAUERNART

1–2 *pullets*
beaten egg
breadcrumbs
parmesan cheese
1 *glass white wine*

4 *oz. mushrooms*
lemon juice
butter
white sauce

Joint the pullets. Mix the cheese and breadcrumbs together. Dip the pullets first in egg then roll in the cheese and breadcrumbs. Fry in butter until brown and tender. Take from the pan, put aside but keep warm.

Fry the mushrooms in the same butter, add the sauce, season and squeeze in a little lemon juice. Stir well, then add the white wine, and if available, one or two beaten egg yolks.

Pour the sauce over the chicken, and serve with a potato salad and crisp fresh lettuce.

CHICKEN WITH RICE
DEUTSCHES HUHN MIT REIS

4 *large boiling fowl*
1 *oz. rice*
1 *oz. flour*
2 *oz. butter*

1–2 *egg yolks*
lemon juice
mixed dried herbs
salt and pepper

Clean and truss the fowl ready for boiling. Place in a large pan with salted boiling water and the herbs. Simmer for two or three hours until it is tender.

In another saucepan bring to the boil some water, to which a little chicken stock has been added. Slowly add

the rice, and cook rapidly for fifteen to twenty minutes.
Strain, and stir in a little of the butter.

Arrange the rice on a large round plate in the shape
of a ring. Take out the fowl, joint, and arrange in the
middle of the rice ring.

From the flour and the rest of the butter make a
white roux. Thin with a little of the chicken stock, and
cook for a few minutes. Flavour with a little lemon
juice, season with salt and pepper, and bind with the
egg yolks. This sauce can be served separately in a
sauceboat, or poured over the chicken.

ROAST CAPERCAILZIE
GEBRATENE AUERHAHN

Take a young bird, trussed and ready for roasting.
Rub with salt, and cover with larding. Place in a baking
tin with a little melted butter and some juniper berries,
and baste from time to time with a sauce made from
three tablespoons of white wine, three tablespoons of
water, and two tablespoons of sour cream with which
one ounce of browned flour has been mixed.

Bake in a moderate oven.

An old bird is treated somewhat differently. It is
rubbed in salt, well larded and then laid in a marinade
of half water, half vinegar, to which has been added a
sprig of thyme, some juniper berries, two tablespoons of
sour cream, and half an ounce of potato flour. Leave for
two or three days.

Dry carefully, rub once more with salt and melted
butter and roast in a moderate oven, basting from time
to time with the marinade. When the bird is tender,

remove from the pan, strain the liquid, thicken if necessary, and pour over the bird before serving.

Serve with an apple compôte.

SADDLE OF HARE
WITH HORSERADISH SAUCE

HASENRÜCKEN MIT MEERRETTICH

1 *saddle of hare*	*wineglass of port wine*
larding	*nutmeg and cinnamon*
1 *teaspoon horseradish*	*salt and pepper*
3 *tablespoons of red currant jelly*	

The saddle must be well larded, rubbed with salt, and braised for twenty or thirty minutes in a covered pan, with enough water to prevent burning. Pour in the wine, the grated nutmeg and cinnamon, and continue cooking until the sauce is reduced to half, and the meat is tender. Stir in the red currant jelly, and finally one heaped teaspoon of grated horseradish.

Serve the hare in its own sauce with plain boiled potatoes, and a green salad.

HARE GIBLETS

HASENPFEFFER

head, heart, lung, stomach of	*mixed dried herbs*
a hare	½ *pint meat stock or gravy*
3 *oz. fat diced bacon*	1 *gill red wine*
1 *oz. flour*	½ *oz. sugar*
1 *oz. chopped onion*	1½ *pints water*

Thoroughly wash the hare giblets, and cook with the

herbs in boiling salted water until tender. Strip the
meat from the bones and cut it into pieces. Fry the
bacon, add the onion and the small pieces of hare meat.
Sprinkle with flour, continue frying until the flour is
browned, then gradually add the stock or gravy. Add
the sugar, and simmer very slowly until everything is
quite soft. Stir in the red wine, and serve hot, with
mashed or riced potatoes.

Some recipes say that the hare giblets should be
washed, blanched, and then laid in a marinade of red
wine, sliced onion, salt and pepper. They are then left
covered with a plate for three to six days, dried, cooked
as above and the marinade is used in the cooking.

VENISON STEAK

REHKOTELETT

2 *lb. venison*	½ *bottle white wine*
1 *stick celery*	1 *oz. truffle*
2 *carrots*	*sugar, salt and pepper*
1 *onion*	½ *teaspoon meat extract*
1 *leek*	4 *slices white crustless*
3 *oz. butter*	*bread*
1 *oz. flour*	

Hammer the meat lightly, skin and wash it. Cut into
thick steaks. Fry the onion in butter, add the other
vegetables, and about one pint of boiling water. Bring
to the boil, add the meat extract, and cook until you
have a well-flavoured stock. Thicken with flour, add the
wine, sugar, salt and pepper, then rub through a fine
wire sieve.

Dip the steaks into this sauce, then fry on both sides in fat until tender, adding the truffle. Cut the bread into triangles and fry until crisp.

Arrange the steaks on a hot plate, cover with the sauce, and garnish with the bread. Serve with chestnuts, glazed or mashed, and sautéed small potato balls.

ROAST DUCK

GEBRATENE ENTE

1 *duck*	*a little potato flour*
8 *good sized apples*	*salt and sugar*

Stuff the duck with the apples, previously peeled. cored and rubbed in sugar. Lay it in a roasting pan with about a quarter of a pint of boiling water (if the bird is lean, lard it first). Roast in a moderate oven until tender, and baste frequently with boiling water.

Take out the duck, strain off surplus fat, and thicken the gravy with the potato flour.

Serve with potato croquettes and orange salad, or with apple purée and red cabbage.

ROAST PIGEON

GEBRATENE TAUBEN

These are treated in much the same manner as poussin, They are usually stuffed, sometimes with a rice pilaff, or with chopped bacon, and even grapes, then rubbed with salt, roasted in melted butter, and basted with either meat stock or wine.

Young birds are jointed, rolled in egg and bread-crumbs, fried, and served with a cold cucumber salad and mashed potatoes.

A mushroom sauce is also recommended with pigeons, and basting when possible with brandy.

PARTRIDGES WITH SAUERKRAUT
REBHÜHNER MIT SAUERKRAUT

2 *large partridges*	*meat stock*
6 *slices of bacon or larding*	*salt and pepper*
2 *lb. sauerkraut*	1 *small chopped onion*
4 *oz. butter*	2 *crushed juniper berries*

Clean the partridges which, for this dish, can be old ones not fit for roasting. Rub them inside and out with salt and pepper. Wrap with bacon. Melt the butter in a heavy saucepan, and fry the birds until they are brown all over. Add the onion, the juniper berries, and about a cup of meat stock. Simmer the birds, and baste from time to time, until they are tender.

Cook the sauerkraut separately. Joint the birds for serving, surround with sauerkraut, and garnish with the bacon. Thicken the gravy with a little flour, and serve it separately or poured over the sauerkraut.

MEAT

FLEISCH

ROAST BEEF GERMAN STYLE

ROSTBRATEN

Bone three pounds of beef, roll and tie with string or fix with skewers. Rub with salt and lard. Place in a greased baking tin with a little boiling water and one chopped onion. Roast in a moderate oven. When the meat begins to brown, baste well with boiling water. Just before it is ready, dot with butter or larding.

Slice thickly, and serve with a thick sour cream sauce.

It is not usual in Germany to serve beef underdone, as it is in England.

BEEF STEAK A LA NELSON

BEEFSTEAK A LA NELSON

1 *fillet of steak*	½ *lb. potatoes*
1 *oz. butter*	*salt and pepper*
½ *oz. chopped onion*	

Melt the butter in a casserole, sauté the potatoes (peeled and sliced) and the onion. Sprinkle with salt and pepper. Grill the steak on both sides, allowing one minute for each side. Add to the potatoes and fry for five minutes over a fierce heat, then gently cook for fifteen minutes. The casserole should be covered during cooking.

Serve the steak in the casserole in which it has been cooked.

BEEF STEWED IN BEER
RINDFLEISCH GEDÄMPFT IN BIER

2 *lb. topside of beef*	2 *carrots*
4 *oz. larding*	2 *oz. mushrooms*
1 *large sliced onion*	*grated lemon rind*
1 *stick celery*	1 *pint bottle beer*
1 *parsnip*	*salt and pepper*

Lightly hammer and lard the meat with half the larding. Slice all the vegetables. Line a casserole with the rest of the larding and place half the vegetables at the bottom. Add the meat, then the remainder of the vegetables. Season well, sprinkle in the grated lemon rind and pour in the beer.

Simmer, tightly covered, for three hours. Take out the meat, keep warm, and thicken the gravy with a flour and water paste.

Serve the meat in its own sauce, and with the vegetables.

BRAISED STEAK
RINDERSCHMORBRATEN

2 *lb. steak*	*capers*
1 *oz. fat chopped bacon or*	*garlic (optional)*
larding	*salt and pepper*
1 *oz. dripping*	1 *small sliced onion*
1 *oz. flour*	*a few pearl onions*

Hammer the steak lightly, then rub with salt and pepper. With a sharp knife make small slits in the meat, and into each slit push a piece of bacon or larding. Roll the meat in seasoned flour, and fry in hot fat. Add the sliced onion. Brown the meat on both sides, then pour in about half a pint of boiling water, and cover the pan tightly.

Leave the meat to simmer until it is very tender, adding if necessary more boiling water.

Take the meat from the pan, slice and keep warm. Thicken the sauce, adding the pearl onions, a little chopped garlic, and the capers. Pour this sauce over the sliced meat, and serve with noodles and a watercress salad.

BRAISED PICKLED BEEF
SAUERBRATEN

1 *lb. topside of beef*	2 *oz. butter*
1 *stick celery*	½ *pint vinegar*
1 *parsnip*	*sour cream*
2 *carrots*	*salt and peppercorns*
1 *onion*	*cloves*
2 *oz. larding*	*bayleaves*

Bring the vinegar, vegetables, salt, peppercorns, bayleaves and cloves to the boil and leave to cool.

Hammer the meat lightly and lay in the marinade. Leave under a wire cover for three days in summer, or five in winter.

Dry the meat with a cloth, and lard it well. Brown on both sides in butter, then add the marinade, strained and diluted with an equal quantity of water. Simmer the meat until it is tender, basting frequently.

Stir the sour cream into the gravy while the meat is still in the pan, and leave the meat still simmering until it has become impregnated with the full flavour of the sauce. Serve the meat and sauce together.

RECHAUFFE OF BEEF WITH EGGS
RINDFLEISCH MIT EIERN

1 *lb. cold beef*	6 *eggs*
2 *oz. butter*	¼ *pint tomato juice*
1 *oz. anchovies*	*salt and pepper*

Slice the meat and lightly sauté in butter, using a casserole. Add salt and pepper, anchovies and the tomato juice. Simmer.

Break the eggs one by one on to the meat, completely covering it, and cook until the egg white has set, and the yolk is cooked through but not hard.

This dish is always cooked on the top of the stove, as oven cooking causes a white film to cover the eggs, and thus spoils its appearance.

COLD BEEF WITH APPLES
RINDFLEISCH MIT ÄPFELN
A north German recipe

1 *lb. cold sliced beef*	½ *pint stock*
2 *oz. butter*	1 *oz. flour*
2 *lb. cooking apples*	*ground cinnamon*
3 *oz. currants*	*grated lemon rind*

Melt the butter and sauté the meat. When it is brown take out and put aside.

Stir the flour into the butter, then gradually add the hot stock. Peel, core and slice the apples and sprinkle with salt, ground cinnamon and grated lemon rind. Add, with the currants, to the stock, and cook until tender. Re-heat the meat for a few minutes. Pour the apple sauce over the meat and serve very hot.

BEEF OLIVES

RINDS ROULADEN

2 *lb. topside of beef* 2 *oz. butter*
4 *oz. fat bacon, cut in strips* *dried mixed herbs*
1 *large chopped onion* *salt and pepper*
1 *sliced gherkin* ½ *pint hot stock*

Cut the meat into thin slices and pound lightly until flattened. Rub with salt and pepper. Place on each slice a strip of bacon, some chopped onion and gherkin, and roll up. Tie with string or fix with a small wooden skewer.

Lightly sauté the rolls in butter until brown. Gradually add the hot stock and season with salt and pepper. Cover, and continue cooking until the meat is tender.

Take the rolls from the pan, thicken the gravy with a flour and water paste, add the herbs, cook for two minutes then pour over the meat rolls.

Serve with noodles or riced potatoes.

Before serving, remove the string or skewer from the meat.

ROAST PORK WITH MADEIRA SAUCE

SCHWEINEBRATEN IN MADEIRASAUCE

2 *lb. roasting pork* *rind of one lemon*
½ *pint white wine* 1 *oz. flour*
¼ *bottle madeira* 1 *tablespoon vinegar*
bayleaves *salt and pepper*

Put the pork into a roasting pan with half a pint of water, the white wine, vinegar, bayleaves, lemon rind, salt and pepper. Bake in a moderate oven. Baste from time to time until the pork is tender. Take from the pan, thicken the sauce with a flour and water paste, add the madeira and strain.

Slice the pork and serve with the sauce poured over it.

To make a crisp crust, remove the pork from the pan when it is tender and leave to get cold. Brush the top with beaten egg yolk, coat with breadcrumbs, moisten with gravy and return to the oven. Continue roasting and basting, until you have a crust half an inch thick.

SILESIAN HEAVEN
SCHLESISCHES HIMMELREICH

1 *lb. pork chops*　　　　　*flour*
½ *lb. dried mixed fruit*　　*butter*

Soak the fruit overnight. Simmer the chops in a little boiling water, until tender. Parboil the fruit, strain, and cook with the chops until it is soft.

Melt the butter in another pan, add the flour, fry for two minutes, stirring all the while. Add the pork and fruit, and the liquid in which they have been cooking. Continue frying for some minutes, then serve with potato or semolina dumplings. The dried fruits used in this recipe are apricots, pears, apples, prunes, etc.

KNUCKLES OF PORK
WITH SAUERKRAUT
EISBEIN MIT SAUERKRAUT

2 *lb. knuckles of pork*
2 *lb. sauerkraut*
1 *stick celery*
1 *parsnip*
2 *carrots*

1 *leek*
2 *peeled and chopped apples*
1 *chopped onion*
salt and pepper

Put the knuckles into a large saucepan, cover with cold water and add the celery, parsnip, carrots, and leek. Season with salt and pepper, bring to the boil, and cook slowly for three hours. Remove the knuckles, pass the stock through a sieve, and bring once more to the boil. Meanwhile, cook the sauerkraut, with the onion and the apples, for at least two hours. Put the knuckles on to a large dish, surrounded by the sauerkraut and with potatoes boiled in their skins. Serve the gravy separately.

PORK CHOPS WITH SOUR CREAM
SCHWEINEKOTELETTS MIT SAURER SAHNE

Trim the chops and rub with salt. Brown in butter on both sides for about ten minutes. Add a gill of sour cream, and simmer for another twenty minutes, or until the meat is tender.

Remove the chops from the pan, thicken the sauce with a little flour and add a few capers.

BREADED PORK CHOPS
SCHWEINEKOTELETTS

1 *lb. pork chops*   *salt*
1 *beaten egg*   *breadcrumbs*

Lightly hammer the chops, then rub with salt. Dip in beaten egg, and roll in breadcrumbs. Fry on both sides in browned butter and serve with slices of lemon.

A variation which gives more flavour is to toss some mixed chopped fresh herbs and sliced shallots in melted butter. Strain, and quickly pour the fat into the beaten egg, stirring all the time, so that the egg does not curdle. Dip the chops into this mixture, then roll in breadcrumbs. Fry in butter on both sides. If there is any of the egg sauce left over, pour it over the chops.

SMOKED PICKLED LOIN OF PORK
KASSELER RIPPESPEER

2 *lb. loin of pork*   1 *oz. potato flour*   *salt and pepper*

Wash the smoked and pickled pork thoroughly, and soak for three hours. Cook in plenty of water until it is tender.

Thicken the liquid in which the pork has been cooking with some potato flour, season and serve separately as a sauce.

Boiled cabbage and plain boiled potatoes are served with this dish.

THE SHOEMAKER'S POT
SCHUSTERPFANNE

1 *lb. lpin of pork*	1½ *lb. pears*
¾ *lb. carrots*	*salt*
1½ *lb. potatoes*	*sugar*

Cut the meat into small pieces, peel and core the pears, and cook together with one gill of water for ten minutes. Add the carrots and potatoes, peeled and sliced, salt, a little sugar, and cook in a covered pot for forty minutes.

PORK LOAF
SCHWEINEFLEISCHKÄSE

1 *lb. cooked pork*	2 *beaten eggs*
1 *lb. cooked liver*	2 *oz. anchovy fillets*
4 *oz. cooked bacon*	4 *shallots*
1 *oz. cooked tongue*	1 *oz. butter*
3 *white rolls*	*salt and pepper*

Pass the pork, liver, and half the bacon twice through the mincer. Soak the rolls and squeeze very dry. Toss the shallots and the anchovies in melted butter, and add to the minced meat. In the same pan lightly fry the bread. Chop the tongue.

Mix all the ingredients to a paste, bind with the eggs, and season with salt and pepper.

Line a baking tin with half the remaining bacon, fill with the paste and cover with the rest of the bacon. Bake for one hour in medium oven.

PIG'S EARS

SCHWEINEOHREN

Soak two pairs of pig's ears for four hours, then simmer gently for two.

Dry carefully and brush with melted butter.

Roll the ears in breadcrumbs, to which grated nutmeg, mixed dried herbs, salt and pepper have been added.

Fry for fifteen minutes in boiling fat.

Serve with caper sauce.

PIG'S EARS WITH SAUERKRAUT

SCHWEINEOHREN MIT SAUERKRAUT

4 *pig's ears*	*salt and pepper*
1 *lb. sauerkraut*	*carraway*

Wash the pig's ears thoroughly then soak in water for four or five hours. Put into a pan together with the sauerkraut, cover with boiling water, and simmer gently for two hours. Season with salt and pepper, and flavour with carraway seeds.

BOILED BACON
WITH BEANS AND PEARS

SCHINKEN MIT BOHNEN UND BIRNEN

Slice about three-quarters of a pound of bacon, and put in the bottom of a pan. On top of the bacon arrange in layers some trimmed and broken French beans, peeled and sliced pears and potatoes. Season with salt and pepper, and add enough water to cover the bottom of the pan. Cook on top of the stove until all the ingredients are tender.

This is the Westphalian version of the same dish:

½ *lb. bacon*	3 *pears*
½ *lb. haricot beans*	2 *large cooking apples*
½ *lb. French beans*	

Soak the haricot beans overnight, and cook next day in a large saucepan until they begin to soften. Peel, core and slice the pears and apples, and slice the bacon. Add to the haricot beans. Cook for another thirty minutes. Season with salt and pepper.

VEAL SCHNITZEL AU NATUREL
KALBSSCHNITZEL

veal fillets　　　　3 *oz. butter*　　　　*sour cream*

Pound the fillets until they are very thin, sprinkle with salt, and rub on one side only with melted butter.

Heat the butter and fry, buttered side only, until the meat begins to brown.

Add the cream and simmer the fillets gently, basting frequently, until they are tender.

Garnish with lemon slices, and squeeze over them a little lemon juice.

Serve with sautéed potatoes and a cold cucumber salad.

BOILED PORK
WITH APPLES AND CARROTS
SCHWEINEFLEISCH MIT MÖHREN UND ÄPFELN

1 *lb. boiling pork*	1 *onion*
1 *lb. carrots*	*sugar, salt and pepper*
½ *lb. apples*	*carraway seeds*
1 *lb. potatoes*	

Cut up the pork, peel and slice the apples, potatoes, and carrots, chop the onion, and arrange in a thick-bottomed saucepan or casserole covered with warm water. Flavour with a few carraway seeds, and season with salt and pepper, and a pinch of sugar. Cover tightly and cook on top of the stove until the meat is tender.

VIENNA SCHNITZEL
WIENER SCHNITZEL

veal fillets	*salt and pepper*
1 *egg*	*butter*
flour and breadcrumbs	

Pound the fillets until thin, roll in seasoned flour, brush with beaten egg and roll in breadcrumbs.

Fry on both sides quickly in hot butter.

Serve very hot with sautéed potatoes and a water-cress or cucumber salad.

In Holstein they serve schnitzels with a fried egg as a garnish. In other parts of the country they use capers, chopped olives, chopped egg whites or sliced gherkins as garnishes.

PICKLED PORK WITH SAUERKRAUT
PÖKELFLEISCH MIT SAUERKRAUT

Soak the pickled pork for several hours, change the water, put into a large saucepan and bring slowly to the boil.

Take the pork from the pot, put on a hot plate, and pour over it some browned butter. Surround with sauerkraut which has been cooked with a little chopped onion.

BRAISED SHIN OF VEAL
GESCHMORTE KALBSHAXE

3 lb. shin of veal
1 stick celery
2 carrots
1 leek
1 onion

1 tomato
mixed dried herbs
bayleaves
salt and pepper
dripping and stock

Leave the veal whole, and fry in dripping until it is brown on all sides. Add all the other ingredients, the vegetables cleaned and chopped, and about one gill of hot stock or water. Cover tightly and leave to simmer slowly until the meat is tender, adding if necessary a little more liquid.

Take the veal from the pan, put on a serving dish and surround with the vegetables. Thicken the liquid, adding as much water or stock as will be needed to make a gravy.

VEAL FRICASSEE
KALBSFRIKASSEE

1 lb. veal
3 oz. butter
1 oz. flour
1 pint stock
mixed herbs
2 egg yolks

1 egg white
4 oz. stewing steak
4 oz. boiling pork
1 chopped onion
salt and pepper
lemon juice

Cut the veal into cubes, roll in flour, and fry in butter. Cover with the stock, add the herbs, salt and pepper, and simmer slowly in a covered casserole. If necessary, more liquid may be added.

Put the steak and pork through a mincer, mix with the onion and bind with one egg yolk. Beat well together, then add the egg white. Shape into small dumplings and poach in boiling water.

Take the veal from the pan, and thicken the sauce in which it has been cooking, adding lemon juice, a beaten egg yolk, salt and pepper. Drain the dumplings and put into the thickened sauce. Return the veal to the pan, re-heat and serve hot.

To improve the flavour add a little anchovy essence to the sauce, also a few sliced and sautéed mushrooms.

RAGOUT OF LIGHTS

LUNGENRAGOUT

This recipe is one of the more popular German winter recipes.

1 *calf's heart and lights*	2 *carrots*
1 *stick of celery*	1 *teaspoon curry powder*
1 *leek*	1 *oz. rice*
1 *onion*	*mixed dried herbs*
1 *parsnip*	1 *oz. butter*
	salt and pepper

Wash the heart and lights and remove the skin and tubes. Cut the lights into pieces, and together with the heart, peeled vegetables (except the onion), seasonings and herbs, put into a pan. Cover with water and cook until tender. Strain off the liquid, and put the meat to one side, keeping it warm.

Melt the butter, fry the onion, the rice and the curry

powder for five minutes, then add the hot liquid. Cook until the rice is tender.

Cut the meat into small pieces and re-heat with the rice. Serve together.

The vegetables are used for flavouring only.

OX-TONGUE
WITH HORSERADISH SAUCE
OCHSENZUNGE MIT MEERRETTICH SAUCE

Actually any kind of cooked tongue will do for this easy yet appetising dish.

Bring half a pint of stock or water to the boil, with about three ounces of horseradish. Simmer for fifteen minutes. Melt one ounce of butter, and mix with it three tablespoons of sour cream, and about one ounce of soft white breadcrumbs. Add this to the horseradish, and stir until the sauce thickens. Strain, beat in one egg yolk and a little made mustard.

Pour over the tongue just before serving.

MEAT CASSEROLE
PICHELSTEINER

1 *lb. boiling pork or beef*	1 *knob celery*
4 *oz. bone marrow*	1 *lb. runner beans*
¾ *lb. carrots*	1 *lb. potatoes*
4 *leeks*	1 *tablespoon chopped parsley*
¼ *pint hot stock*	

Soak the marrow for two hours before using, then cut into small pieces. Cut the meat into pieces and put in the bottom of a saucepan. Prepare all the vegetables and cut into small pieces. Add half the bone marrow to the pan, then the vegetables and chopped parsley, and the remainder of the marrow. Season well with salt and pepper, pour in about a quarter of a pint of hot stock, and simmer gently for one and a half hours.

KÖNIGSBERGER MEAT BALLS
KÖNIGSBERGER KLOPS

1 *lb. stewing meat*	*salt and pepper*
4 *oz. crustless white bread*	*juice of half a lemon*
2 *oz. suet*	1 *oz. chopped capers*
1 *large grated onion*	4 *chopped anchovies*
1 *egg*	*bayleaves and clove*
1 *oz. cooked and riced potato*	

Pass the meat and suet twice through a mincer. Sauté the onion and add to the meat. Soak the bread and squeeze it dry. Work bread, potatoes, meat and onion to a smooth paste, adding the capers and the anchovies, and bind with the egg.

Break off pieces and shape into balls, somewhat larger than a golf ball.

Bring some water to the boil in a large saucepan with the bayleaves, clove and lemon juice. Carefully arrange the meat balls in the bottom of the pan, bring once more slowly to the boil, then simmer gently for thirty minutes.

Take the balls out of the pan with a draining spoon, and put to one side. Thicken the stock in which they have been cooked with flour, and add a little anchovy paste. Cook for two or three minutes, then return the meat balls. Re-heat, and serve together in a deep dish.

Serve with rice or boiled potatoes, and caper sauce.

STUFFED VEAL
GEFÜLLTES KALBSBRUST

2 lb. breast of veal
½ lb. mutton
½ lb. fat minced pork
1 white roll
1 small grated onion

1 egg
1 oz. butter
mixed herbs
lemon rind
salt and pepper

Remove the bones and tendons, and flatten the veal with a rolling pin or a cutlet bat. Season with salt and pepper.

Put the mutton and pork twice through a mincer. Soak the bread, squeeze well and mix with the minced meat. Melt the butter, and lightly fry the onion in it. Knead the minced meat, bread, onion, egg, and mixed herbs to a paste and spread over the veal. Roll the veal, and secure it either by sewing or with large skewers.

Sprinkle with flour, and fry in the same butter in which the onion was fried. Add boiling water or stock and simmer until tender.

MUTTON WITH BEANS
HAMMELFLEISCH MIT BOHNEN

1½ lb. mutton
1½ lb. runner beans
1 lb. potatoes

chopped parsley
salt and pepper
2 large chopped onions
capers

Cut the meat into small pieces. Put in the bottom of a saucepan, cover with the onions, trimmed beans, and potatoes peeled and thickly sliced. Pour in four or five tablespoons of water, and one ounce of butter (unless the meat is fat). Season with salt and pepper, flavour with capers, and sprinkle with chopped parsley. Bring quickly to the boil, then simmer until the meat is tender.

This dish can also be prepared with large sliced tomatoes and leeks. Another favourite vegetable used in this way is the kohlrabi.

MUTTON COOKED WITH ONIONS
ZWIEBELFLEISCH MIT KÜMMEL

2 *lb. stewing mutton* ¼ *teaspoon of carraway seeds*
1 *lb. sliced onions* *salt and pepper*
1 *oz. flour*

Put the meat into a saucepan with just enough water to cover. Add the onions, salt, pepper, and carraway seeds. Simmer gently until the meat is tender and brown, shaking the pan from time to time to prevent burning. Thicken the liquid with flour, and serve the meat covered in the onions, and with mashed potatoes.

BRAISED LIVER
GEDÄMFTE LEBER

1 *lb. liver* *a little truffle*
4 *oz. butter* 1 *tablespoon wine vinegar*
1 *glass white wine* 1 *chopped onion*
1 *strip lemon rind* *bayleaves*
½ *pint stock* *salt and peppercorns*

Skin the liver, and gently sauté in butter. Cover with stock, wine and vinegar. Add the onion, truffle, bayleaves, salt, peppercorns, and lemon rind. Allow to simmer, with the pan tightly covered, until the liver is tender. Take out the liver, thicken the gravy, and pour over the liver when serving.

LIVER LOAF
LEBERKÄSE

1½ *lb. sliced liver*
½ *lb. chopped fat bacon*
1 *chopped onion*
2 *white rolls*

salt and pepper
½ *lb. larding*
marjoram

Soak the rolls in milk or water and squeeze dry. Mix the bacon, liver, and onion together, and put twice through a mincer. Flavour with marjoram and season with salt and pepper. Line a tin evenly with larding, then pack firmly with the minced liver paste. Bake in a moderate oven for one hour.

Serve with a tomato or caper sauce.

Instead of lining the tin with larding you can make a pastry case, adding grated cheese to the pastry while mixing.

RAGOUT OF TONGUE
ZUNGENRAGOUT

2 *cooked calves' tongues or*
    half a pickled ox-tongue
½ *lb. sausage meat*
1 *beaten egg yolk*
1 *oz. parmesan cheese*
½ *lb. mushrooms (champignons)*
12 *green olives*
6 *shallots*
2 *oz. butter*

2 *tablespoons tomato purée*
½ *pint stock*
meat extract
Worcester or soya sauce
a dozen croûtons
salt, pepper and sugar
wineglass of red wine
1 *chopped onion*
1 *oz. flour*

Skin the tongue, thickly slice, and arrange in a greased casserole. Put the sausage meat through a mincer, then mix with the cheese and egg yolk. Break off pieces and roll into small dumplings. Poach in boiling water for five minutes. Arrange between the slices of tongue.

Slice the mushrooms and fry them in butter with the onion, and the shallots. Stone and slice the olives. Add shallots, mushrooms, onion and olives to the other ingredients in the casserole.

Stir the flour into the tomato purée. Add the red wine, stock and meat extract. Bring to the boil. Flavour with the Worcester or soya sauce, then pour into the casserole.

Bake in a moderate oven for about twenty minutes. Garnish with croûtons, and serve with plain boiled potatoes tossed in butter, and a watercress salad.

STEWED OX-TONGUE WITH SAUCE
RINDERZUNGE MIT SAUCE

1 *ox-tongue*	2 *carrots*
2 *oz. mushrooms (champignons)*	*wineglass of madeira*
1 *stick celery*	½ *oz. raisins*
1 *parsnip*	1 *dessertspoon capers*
1 *onion*	

Soak the tongue overnight. Wash it, and put in a pan with enough water to cover. Bring slowly to the boil, with the vegetables, cleaned and chopped, madeira and raisins. Keep the saucepan tightly covered and simmer for three hours. When the tip of the tongue is tender to the touch it is ready, and will skin without difficulty.

Drain the tongue thoroughly. Remove the skin and gristle, and cut into medium thick slices.

FOR THE SAUCE:

Strain off the vegetables and rub through a sieve. Return to the stock, thicken if necessary with a little potato flour, add the capers, and bring once more to the boil. Serve the sliced tongue in this sauce.

BAKED APPLES STUFFED WITH LIVER
ÄPFEL MIT LEBERFÜLLE

8 *large cooking apples*	*2 oz. pork*
goose liver	*marjoram and thyme*
1 oz. butter	*wineglass of white wine*

Wash the apples and scoop out the centres. Put the pork, the scooped-out apple, liver, thyme and marjoram through a mincer. Stuff the apples with this mixture. Grease a dish with butter, arrange the apples in it, add the wine, cover and bake in the oven for about twenty minutes.

Serve with either roast pork or goose.

BRAISED KIDNEYS
GESCHMORTE NIEREN

¾ *lb. kidneys*	*1 tablespoon vinegar*
butter or bacon fat	*salt*
1 chopped onion	*1 oz. flour*
¼ *pint sour cream or buttermilk*	

Remove all the fat and skin from the kidneys, and cut into very thin slices. Sauté the onion in butter or bacon fat until it is a golden-brown colour, add the kidneys, fry for a few minutes then add the cream or buttermilk. Season with salt, and simmer gently for one hour.

Mix the flour and vinegar together and thicken the kidney gravy.

Serve with mashed potatoes.

MEAT BALLS WITH MUSHROOMS
FLEISCHKLÖSSE MIT PILZEN

1 *lb. raw meat*	1 *oz. butter*
½ *lb. sliced mushrooms*	1 *small chopped onion*
1 *whole egg*	¼ *pint white wine*
2 *egg yolks*	¼ *pint stock*
1 *white roll*	*salt, pepper and parsley*
1 *oz. flour*	*juice of one lemon*

Melt the butter, stir in the flour, brown, then add the stock. Cook for two minutes. Add the mushrooms and simmer until they are tender. Beat the egg yolks with the lemon juice, and pour over the mushrooms. Continue simmering, but do not allow to boil.

Put the meat twice through the mincer, the second time with the onion. Soak the roll and squeeze it dry. Mix with the minced meat. Season with salt and pepper, bind with the egg and knead to a smooth paste. Break off pieces and form into balls. Drop into boiling water and cook until the meat is done. (Cooking time varies according to the quality and type of meat.) Drain, add to the mushrooms and simmer a while in

the sauce. Add the wine, and the chopped parsley just
before serving.

WILD BOAR CUTLETS
WILDSCHWEINRÜCKEN

2 *lb. wild boar cutlets*	*salt*
3 *juniper berries*	*flour*
buttermilk	

Leave the cutlets for three days lying in buttermilk.
Dry with a cloth, rub with salt and pounded juniper
berries. Roast or grill the cutlets. If roasting, put into a
pan with a little boiling water, and baste from time to
time with the buttermilk. When the meat is tender,
thicken the sauce with flour, and serve the cutlets in
their own sauce.

BEAR FILLET IN BURGUNDY
BÄRENFILET IN BURGUNDER

1 *fillet of bear (about 7 lb.)*	5 *juniper berries*
onions, parsnips, celery	2 *bottles of burgundy*
and carrots	*larding*

Bear meat, like venison, should be hung for several days
before using. Some cooks also put it in a marinade of
spiced tarragon vinegar.

Cut out all the sinews and nerves; bear meat must
always be handled carefully, otherwise the meat is
injured. Lard well, and rub with salt and pounded
juniper berries. Place in a baking tin, surrounded by
the vegetables. Pour over the burgundy, and half a pint

of boiling water or stock. Roast for four to five hours, basting frequently.

Take the meat from the pan. Rub the vegetables through a sieve, stir back into the gravy and serve separately as a sauce. It is, in Germany, usual to eat sauerkraut with bear.

This is perhaps rather a frivolous recipe, but I think that it is always nice to know what to do with the unexpected.

STUFFED BREAST OF LAMB
GEFÜLLTE HAMMELBRUST

3 *lb. breast of lamb*	*red wine or sour cream*
¾ *lb. mushrooms*	*flour*
1 *large onion*	

Bone the lamb, and stuff with a mixture of chopped mushrooms and onion. Sprinkle with salt and pepper, roll and tie with string or secure with skewers.

Rub the outside with melted butter, place in a baking tin, and when the meat begins to brown baste with boiling water or stock.

When the meat is tender, take it from the pan and thicken the gravy. Add either red wine or sour cream to flavour. Serve the meat and sauce separately.

GERMAN BEEFSTEAKS (Hamburgers)
DEUTSCHES BEEFSTEAK

1 *lb. minced raw beef*	1 *small chopped onion*
2 *oz. suet*	2 *oz. butter*
1 *stale milk roll*	

Soak the roll and squeeze it dry. Put the meat and the suet through a mincer, then mix with the bread. Knead to a paste, and shape into round flat cakes. With a knife mark the top criss-cross fashion. Brown the butter and fry the steaks. Do not allow them to overcook as they easily become dried out. At the same time fry the onion.

Sprinkle the steaks with salt and pepper when serving, and cover with the fried onion.

BEAVER'S TAIL

BIBERSCHWANZ

This is considered by many Germans a delicacy. It is sometimes eaten as an accompaniment to steamed beaver meat or qualifies as a separate dish garnished with thick slices of lemon.

1 *beaver's tail*	*butter or other fat for frying*
1 *beaten egg*	*vinegar*
brown breadcrumbs	

Skin, wash, clean and dry the tail. Cook in half water and vinegar until it is tender. Remove it from the pan, cut into suitable pieces, dip in beaten egg and roll in breadcrumbs. Fry in hot butter or other fat until a golden brown.

SAUERKRAUT

SAUERKRAUT

SAUERKRAUT is probably the best known of all German vegetables. Generally it is easier to buy ready made, but for those housewives who like to do things for themselves, I have given this recipe. It should, of course, be made in a large quantity, otherwise there would be no point in bothering at all.

50 *lb. cabbage*   *vinegar*   2 *lb. salt*

Rub a clean wooden tub with vinegar and cover the bottom with the outside leaves of large white cabbages. Shred the cabbage, mix with the salt and pack into the tub until it is filled. Cover with more cabbage leaves, sprinkle freely once more with salt, then spread with a damp cloth. Cover with a lid slightly smaller than the top of the tub, and weigh it down. Leave for three weeks.

From time to time it will be necessary to stir the cabbage with a clean wooden stick in order to let the gas escape. When the cabbage has fermented the tub must be placed in a cooler place. Great care should be taken that the air does not reach the cabbage.

SAUERKRAUT WITH WHITE WINE

SAUERKRAUT MIT WEISSWEINE

Simmer about one pound of sauerkraut with two ounces

of butter, and enough water to prevent burning. When it has been cooking for thirty minutes add half a pint of white wine and continue cooking until tender.

Sauerkraut is also served with lightly poached oysters.

Another method is to bake sauerkraut in a casserole with bacon and apple for three hours in a moderate oven.

Sour cream is poured over the sauerkraut before cooking to prevent it from becoming dry.

SAUERKRAUT
SAUERKRAUT

1 *lb. sauerkraut*	½ *teaspoon salt*
¼ *teaspoon carraway seeds*	*black pepper*

Drain the sauerkraut, put into a pan with boiling water, and cook slowly from one to two hours. Season with salt and pepper and flavour with carraway seeds. Tinned sauerkraut takes the same time to cook.

SAUERKRAUT WITH APPLES
SAUERKRAUT MIT ÄPFELN

1 *lb. sauerkraut*	1 *teaspoon sugar*
3 *cooking apples*	½ *oz. flour*
1 *sliced onion*	*salt and pepper*
1 *oz. fat*	1 *raw grated potato*
¼ *teaspoon carraway seeds*	

Melt the fat in a large saucepan, add the sauerkraut,

fry for two minutes, then add boiling water to cover. Add the apples, peeled and sliced, the onion, and sugar. Cook very slowly until the sauerkraut is tender. Add the potato, and the flour, previously mixed with a little of the cooking water. Add salt, pepper, and carraway seeds, and cook for a further ten minutes.

FRANKFURTER SAUSAGES WITH SAUERKRAUT
FRANKFURTER WÜRSTCHEN MIT SAUERKRAUT

Slowly cook the sauerkraut, with a few carraway seeds, salt and pepper for two hours.

In another pan bring some water to the boil, drop in the sausages, and cook for ten minutes. Drain and serve with the sauerkraut.

In winter serve boiled potatoes with this dish, in summer, potato salad.

MIXED VEGETABLES (Leipzig Style)
LEIPZIGER ALLERLEI

½ lb. shelled green peas
½ lb. fresh young carrots
½ lb. French beans broken
　into halves
1 cauliflower

¼ lb. sliced mushrooms
4 oz. butter
1 pint stock
1 tablespoon flour
small bread dumplings

All the vegetables after being washed and prepared are cooked separately. When they are tender, strain, and toss lightly for a few minutes in butter. Keep hot. Sauté

the mushrooms in butter, take from the pan, but reserve
the butter. Arrange all the vegetables and the mushrooms on a large plate with the cauliflower, divided into
flowerets, in the centre.

Add a little flour to the mushroom butter, fry for
two or three minutes, then gradually thin with some of
the vegetable water. Cook until the sauce is smooth,
and season with salt and paprika pepper.

This dish is sometimes garnished with shrimps and
served with small dumplings.

Other vegetables may, of course, be used for this
dish. Kohlrabi and asparagus are especially popular in
Germany when in season. Sometimes fried chipped
potatoes are also added.

STUFFED CABBAGE

GEFÜLLTER KOHL

1 *large firm cabbage*	1 *teaspoon capers*
½ *lb. raw minced meat*	*ground nutmeg*
1 *onion*	*tomato purée*
1 *rasher bacon*	*salt and pepper*
1 *teaspoon anchovy essence*	*flour*

Remove the spoiled outer leaves of the cabbage before
blanching it for ten minutes in boiling salted water.
Strain and cool. Cut off the top, and carefully scoop out
the centre.

Chop the onion, and mix with the meat, anchovy
essence, capers, salt and pepper, and fill the scooped-
out cabbage with this mixture. Replace the top, screen
with skewers, and wrap in large white cloth. Gather up

the ends of the cloth, and tie firmly with string. Put into a saucepan of boiling salted water. Add to the cooking water a little grated nutmeg and tomato purée, and cook for forty-five minutes.

Strain the cabbage. Dice the bacon and fry until it is crisp. Add flour to the bacon fat, brown, then gradually add enough cabbage water to make a thin sauce. Season with salt and pepper and serve separately.

STUFFED CABBAGE LEAVES
KOHLROULADEN

1 *large cabbage*	*paprika*
½ *lb. minced meat*	*fat for frying*
1 *beaten egg*	¼ *pint of water*
1 *roll*	*sour cream*
1 *chopped onion*	*flour*

Discard the outer wilted leaves, and place the cabbage in a pan of salted boiling water. Cook until the leaves will separate easily. Drain and leave to cool.

Soak the roll and squeeze dry and work with the minced meat, chopped onion, egg and paprika, to a paste.

Separate the cabbage leaves and carefully cut out the thick middle ribs. Place a dessertspoonful of the minced meat in the middle of each leaf. Fold into neat rolls, tucking in the ends and sides, and tie with cotton. Drain, and dry with a cloth.

Melt the fat in a pan and brown the rolls on all sides. Add the water, cover, and simmer for one and a half hours. Take out the rolls, and thicken the liquid with flour and sour cream. Season with salt and pepper.

Remove the cotton from the rolls, and arrange in a deep serving dish. Pour the sauce over the rolls before serving.

CREAMED SPINACH

SPINAT

2 *lb. spinach*	1–2 *tablespoons of breadcrumbs*
1 *oz. butter*	*chopped chives*
half a chopped onion	*cream or top of milk*

Pick off the stalks and wash the spinach in cold water until free from grit. Put into a pan with hardly any water, and sprinkle with salt. Leave uncovered, and cook slowly without letting it boil. Remove the spinach from the pan and chop finely, or rub through a sieve.

Melt the butter in the same pan, fry the onion, but do not brown, then add the spinach and fry gently for ten minutes. Add the bread crumbs, flavour with chives, and stir in enough cream or top of milk to make a thick creamy sauce.

RED CABBAGE

ROTKOHL

1 *large red cabbage*	1 *chopped onion*
2 *tablespoons fat*	1 *teaspoon sugar*
(preferably dripping)	*a few cloves*
4 *chopped apples*	1 *wineglass of red wine*

Melt the fat in a thick-bottomed saucepan, then add the cabbage, finely shredded, the apples, onion, sugar, cloves, and just enough vinegar or water to prevent burning. Simmer for two hours, add the wine, and continue slowly cooking until the liquid is reduced to nothing.

BAVARIAN CABBAGE
BAYRISCHES KRAUT

1 *large white cabbage*	1 *teaspoon brown sugar*
1 *large finely chopped onion*	1 *oz. dripping*
½ *pint white wine*	*salt and pepper*

Remove the outer leaves of the cabbage, and divide it into four. Cut out the thick ribs and shred the cabbage finely.

Melt the fat in a saucepan, and add the onion and lightly fry. Stir in the sugar, then the wine, previously warmed. Add the cabbage, salt and pepper and cook until tender.

Serve with chestnuts and fat roast meat, such as pork.

STUFFED POTATOES
GEFÜLLTE KARTOFFELN

2 *lb. potatoes*	¼ *pint sour cream*
4 *oz. chopped ham*	1 *beaten egg*
1 *chopped onion*	½ *pint stock*

Choose large well-formed potatoes. Scrub them, but do not peel, and cook in salted water until almost soft.

Cut each potato into half, and scoop out the centres. Mix the scooped-out potato with the ham, onion, beaten egg and half the sour cream. Stuff the potatoes with this mixture.

Put the potatoes into a greased baking tin, add the stock and the rest of the cream. Cover, and bake in a moderate oven for thirty minutes. Serve the gravy separately.

POTATOES WITH BECHAMEL SAUCE
KARTOFFELN MIT BÉCHAMELSAUCE

1 *lb. potatoes (boiled in their*   2 *oz. parmesan cheese*
  skins)   1 *oz. butter*
¾ *pint Béchamel sauce*

Peel and slice the potatoes and mix with the Béchamel sauce (see page 151). If the potatoes are too floury, add just a little milk. Melt the butter in a casserole, sprinkle with some of the cheese, add the potatoes, sprinkle with the rest of the cheese and bake in the oven until they are a golden brown.

MASHED POTATOES WITH TRUFFLE
KARTOFFEL BREI MIT TRÜFFELN

1 *lb. potatoes*   1 *glass white wine*
1 *oz. truffle*   1 *tablespoon sour cream*

Cook the potatoes in salted water until soft, and press through a ricer. Chop the truffle and warm in a saucepan with the wine. Add the cream, stir, then add the potatoes. Re-heat very slowly to bring out the full flavour of the truffle, then beat until the potatoes are creamy.

Serve with roast pork, ham or tongue cooked in a madeira sauce.

BROWN POTATOES
BRAUNE KARTOFFELN

2 *lb. potatoes*	1 *small sour gherkin*
4 *oz. fat*	1 *oz. mixed raisins*
3 *oz. flour*	1 *oz. currants*
1 *large chopped onion*	¼ *pint stock*
	salt and pepper

Wash, peel and boil the potatoes. Strain and keep warm. Fry the fat and flour to a brown roux and gradually add the stock. Add the onion, raisins and currants, gherkin and seasoning. Slice the potatoes and throw them into the sauce, leaving them until they have absorbed it all and become quite brown.

Serve the potatoes with the currants, raisins, gherkin and onions.

POTATO PANCAKES
KARTOFFELPUFFER

1 *lb. raw grated potatoes*	1 *egg*
2 *oz. cooked potatoes*	*salt*

Mix together the cooked and raw potatoes with the egg

and salt. Stir well. Heat a little fat in a frying pan and drop tablespoons of the mixture in the pan. Fry on both sides until brown and crisp.

These pancakes are also made with grated raw potatoes to which flour is added. To one pound of raw potato add four ounces of flour. Season and mix with egg as on previous page.

Serve potato pancakes with mixed stewed fruit, as in Northern Germany, or as in Westphalia, with sliced cooked apples. They should be eaten as soon as they come out of the pan.

CARROTS RHINELAND STYLE
MÖHREN (RHEINLÄNDISCH)

1 *lb. carrots*	2 *sliced onions*
½ *lb. peeled and sliced apples*	*salt, sugar and pepper*

Scrape the carrots and slice lengthwise. Cook in boiling water with a little sugar until almost tender. Fry the onions in a little fat until golden brown, add the carrots, and the water in which they have been cooking. Add the apples, and cook until all the ingredients are soft. Season with salt and pepper, and just before serving squeeze over a little lemon juice.

STUFFED ARTICHOKE BOTTOMS
ARTISCHOCKENBÖDEN

Tinned artichoke bottoms do very well for this dish.

If, however, you use the fresh globe artichoke, cook in a pan with boiling water until tender, then carefully remove all the leaves and the choke. This leaves the *fond* or 'bottom'.

Before stuffing, see that the artichokes are hot. For the filling:

Lightly fry some chopped onion, and sliced mushroom in a pan until tender, and mix with a Béchamel sauce (see page 151). Fill the artichoke bottoms with this mixture and bake in the oven for a short while.

Another German filling is made with onion purée. Boil as many onions as required until soft enough to rub through a sieve. Melt a little butter in a pan, and add enough flour to make a white roux. Add the onion purée, season with salt and pepper, and cook for a few minutes. Fill the artichoke bottoms, sprinkle with grated cheese, and bake in the oven for ten minutes. An egg beaten into the onion purée is a great improvement.

HOPS WITH MUSHROOMS
HOPFENKEIME

Hops are frequently eaten in Southern Germany. Often they are cooked as asparagus, and served with melted butter, or with a Hollandaise sauce. They have a light, bitter flavour, which is nevertheless piquant. I have read that hops were also quite popular as a vegetable in England at one time.

½ *lb. hop shoots*   1 *oz. butter*
½ *lb. mushrooms*

Cook the hops in boiling salted water until tender, then strain, and drain completely dry on a sieve. Sauté lightly in butter, then cover the pan with a lid, and leave the hops to steam in butter for fifteen minutes. While the hops are cooking, lightly fry the mushrooms, and when tender serve the two vegetables together.

FRENCH BEANS WITH EGG SAUCE

GRÜNE BOHNEN MIT EIERSAUCE

1 *lb. French beans*	1 *small chopped onion*
1 *oz. flour*	*juice of half a lemon*
1 *egg*	*chopped parsley*
½ *oz. butter*	*salt and pepper*

Break the beans into halves and cook in boiling water until tender. While the beans are cooking, make a brown roux with the butter and flour, and add the chopped onion. Season with salt and pepper, and add a little of the bean water. Transfer the beans to this sauce about ten minutes before they are ready.

Beat the egg with the lemon juice and chopped parsley and pour over the beans just before serving.

FRENCH BEANS WITH ONION SAUCE

GRÜNE BOHNEN MIT ZWIEBELSAUCE

1 *lb. French beans*	½ *pint milk*
1 *oz. flour*	*salt and pepper*
1 *small chopped onion*	

Trim, and break the beans into halves. Cook in boiling water until tender, using as little water as possible.

While they are cooking, simmer the chopped onion in the milk, season with salt and pepper, and when the onions are tender thicken the milk with flour. Strain the beans, and cook with the onions for just a few minutes before serving.

GREEN BEANS WITH A SWEET-SOUR SAUCE AND BACON

GRUENE BOHNEN MIT SPECK (SAUERSUESS)

1 *lb. green beans*	1 *dessertspoon sugar*
¼ *lb. bacon scraps*	*salt and pepper*
1 *tablespoon vinegar or lemon*	1 *dessertspoon flour*

Wash and if necessary string the beans. Break them into short lengths. Cook in salted, boiling water for ten minutes. Chop the bacon into small pieces and fry in a hot pan until crisp. Remove the bacon from the pan and keep it hot. In the bacon fat fry the onion, finely chopped, until a light brown. Sprinkle the flour over the onion, let it cook for two or three minutes, stirring all the time; then add enough hot liquid from the beans to make a smooth sauce. Add salt and pepper to taste, the vinegar and sugar, and stir well. Strain the beans and put them in the sauce. Continue cooking until the beans are tender, shaking the pan from time to time to prevent burning. Serve the beans in their sauce and sprinkle over them the hot pieces of bacon.

HARICOT BEANS WITH APPLES
BOHNEN MIT ÄPFELN

2 *lb. cooking apples*   1 *lemon*
1 *lb. white haricot beans*   *salt*
2 *oz. butter*

Soak the beans overnight and cook next morning in
boiling salted water until they are soft. Peel and core
the apples and cut into quarters. Cook them in a little
water and one ounce of butter, but do not allow them
to become too soft. Combine the apples and beans.
Flavour with the juice of one lemon and pour over them
the rest of the butter—melted and browned.

In some parts of Germany, fried bacon, cut into small
pieces, and slices of fried onion, are also added.

BROAD BEANS
GROSSE BOHNEN

butter   *salt and chopped parsley*
broad beans (with pods)

Shell the beans and sauté in butter. Add a very little
water, season, and simmer until tender. Sprinkle
liberally with parsley before serving.

BEANS WITH PEARS
GRÜNE BOHNEN MIT BIRNEN

1 *lb. runner beans*   1 *oz. butter*
1 *lb. pears*   *salt and pepper*

Trim the beans, and cut—not slice—into small pieces. Put into a pan with melted butter, then add the peeled and cored pears. Add boiling water to cover and cook until both are tender.

BROAD BEANS WITH BACON
GROSSE BOHNEN MIT SPECK

½ *lb. bacon*   *flour and chopped parsley*
2 *lb. shelled broad beans*   *salt and pepper*

The bacon can be cooked either in one piece or sliced. Use just enough water to prevent burning and cook until the bacon is almost tender. Throw in the beans, season and continue cooking until both bacon and beans are tender. Thicken the liquid with flour, and sprinkle liberally with chopped parsley. Potatoes may also be cooked together with the beans and bacon, in which case more water is needed, but no flour to thicken the water. The potatoes and beans are added at the same time.

YELLOW BEANS WITH PEARS
WACHSBOHNEN MIT BIRNEN

1 *lb. yellow beans*   *juice of half a lemon*
1 *lb. pears*   1 *tablespoon of sugar*
1 *oz. flour*   *salt and pepper*
1 *oz. butter*

Trim the beans, peel and chop the pears, and put both

into a pan with just enough water to cover. Add the
sugar, salt, pepper and lemon juice. Cook until tender.
Strain off the liquid. In another saucepan make a roux
from the flour and butter, and cook for two or three
minutes. Add the strained liquid, stir well and return
to the beans and pears. Simmer for a few minutes and
serve the beans and pears in the sauce.

These yellow beans are grown a lot in Germany, and
can be grown in this country. I think that they are
sometimes called the 'Golden Butter Bean' in English
seed lists. They look rather like fat French beans, and
are cooked whole.

STUFFED TOMATOES
GEFÜLLTE TOMATEN

7 *large firm tomatoes*   2 *egg yolks*
2 *oz. butter*   2 *tablespoons breadcrumbs*
½ *lb. chopped mushrooms*   2 *tablespoons olive oil*
2 *tablespoons chopped parsley* *salt and pepper*
1 *small chopped onion*

Cut off the tops of the tomatoes and scoop out the
centres. Melt the butter in a pan, add the mushrooms,
onion, parsley, egg yolks, breadcrumbs, salt and pepper.
Scramble them all together, simmer for about ten
minutes, and then while still hot, fill the tomatoes.
Replace the tops. Heat the oil in a flat baking dish, and
place the stuffed tomatoes in it. Baste them once with a
little olive oil, sprinkle with breadcrumbs and bake in
a hot oven for about fifteen to twenty minutes.

TOMATO FILLING I

1 *oz. butter*
1 *oz. flour*
¼ *pint of milk*
1 *egg yolk*

2 *oz. chopped raw bacon*
1 *teaspoon chopped chives*
salt and pepper

Make a white sauce from the flour, butter and milk. Season with salt and pepper. Add the egg (previously beaten with a little of the milk), the scooped out tomato, bacon and chives. Cook for a few minutes then stuff into the tomato cases.

TOMATO FILLING II

2 *white rolls*
¼ *pint milk*
2 *oz. butter*

1 *small chopped onion*
mixed dried herbs
salt and paprika

Cut the rolls into pieces and soak in milk. Melt the butter and lightly fry the onion. Add the soaked bread and the milk, and simmer for a few minutes on a very low heat. Add the seasoning and herbs, and the scooped out tomato, mix well, and when quite cooked, stuff into tomato cases.

STUFFED ONIONS
GEFÜLLTE ZWIEBELN

8–10 *large onions*
½ *lb. minced meat*
½ *pint stock*
sugar, herbs, carraway seeds

tomato purée
chopped parsley
salt and pepper

Peel the onions and boil in slightly salted water for ten minutes. Drain and keep warm. Season the meat, add herbs, sugar and carraway seeds (to taste), and mix with sufficient tomato purée to make a thick paste. Scoop out the centres of the drained onions, and fill with the meat mixture. Arrange the onions in a casserole, and add enough water to come half-way up the onions. Bake in a moderate oven for thirty minutes.

Either raw or cooked meat can be used for this recipe. If raw meat is used, it is advisable to cook it a little before stuffing it into the onions.

STUFFED CUCUMBER
GEFÜLLTE GURKEN

2 *medium cucumbers*	¼ *pint cream*
2 *slices white bread*	*chopped dill*
½ *lb. minced cooked meat*	*salt and pepper*
bacon rashers	

Thinly peel the cucumbers and cut off both ends. With a sharp knife scoop out the middle. Steep the cucumbers for one minute in boiling water, then quickly plunge into cold water. Drain well.

Soak the bread and squeeze it dry. Mix it with the meat, flavour with chopped dill and season with salt and pepper. Stuff tightly into the cucumbers. Wrap slices of fat bacon round the cucumbers and place in a flat casserole. Put enough water or stock into the casserole almost to cover, and bake slowly in a moderate oven for one hour.

Drain the cucumbers, and put on a hot dish. Thicken

with a little flour the liquid in which they were cooked.
Add the cream. Pour this sauce over the cucumbers,
and serve with slices of lemon.

VEGETABLE MARROW WITH APPLES

KÜRBIS MIT ÄPFELN

1 *medium marrow*	*lemon rind*
1 *lb. peeled and sliced apples*	*salt and sugar to taste*
ground cinnamon	

Peel the marrow, slice, and remove all the seeds. Cook
in a small quantity of boiling water for ten minutes.
Add the apples, cinnamon, sugar, salt, and lemon rind,
and cook until both are soft.

To vary this recipe: fry two ounces of chopped,
rather fat bacon, in a saucepan and add one large
chopped onion. Fry until the onion is a golden brown
colour, then add the peeled, seeded and chopped marrow and a little water. Continue then as above but
omitting the cinnamon.

Pumpkin can be cooked in exactly the same way.

MUSHROOMS
WITH ONIONS AND CREAM

PFEFFERLINGE MIT ZWIEBELN UND SAHNE

½ *lb. mushrooms*	¼ *pint sour cream*
3 *oz. butter*	*flour*
1 *chopped onion*	*salt and pepper*

Lightly fry the onions in butter for about ten minutes, then add the mushrooms, sliced in halves. Continue frying until onions and mushrooms are tender. Thicken the cream with a little flour, season with salt and pepper and add to the mushrooms and onions a few minutes before serving.

KOHLRABI
KOHLRABI

This vegetable is not very well known in England. It is rather like the turnip, both leaves and root are eaten, and the vegetable should always be pulled while still young and tender. Peeling is not necessary.

Cook the kohlrabi tops as you would spinach. Boil until tender, then pass through a sieve. Make a brown roux, add the tops, a little cream, salt and pepper. Stir and cook until the tops are creamed.

Cook the root of the kohlrabi separately in salted water until tender. Drain and slice, and serve with the creamed kohlrabi tops.

Creamed kohlrabi tops make excellent fillings for pancakes, or as a basis for a dish of poached eggs.

Kohlrabi is also often served in Hamburg with a plain white sauce.

STUFFED KOHLRABI
GEFÜLLTER KOHLRABI

Scrape the kohlrabi, cut off the tops, and scoop out the centres.

Make a stuffing from some minced meat, chopped fried bacon, two chopped anchovies, a little grated lemon rind, and one egg. Fill the centres of the kohlrabis, replace the tops as lids and fix firmly with small wooden sticks.

Cook slowly until tender in salted boiling water.

The scooped out portion of the kohlrabis can be cooked with the leaves, mashed and served with the stuffed kohlrabi.

LEEKS IN WHITE WINE

PORREE MIT WEISWEIN

About 8 *leeks*	*breadcrumbs*
1 *glass white wine*	*salt and pepper*
1 *oz. butter*	

Use the white part only of the leeks. Sauté for two or three minutes in half the butter, add the wine and simmer until tender. Brown the breadcrumbs in the remaining butter and sprinkle over the leeks when serving.

TRUFFLES IN BURGUNDY

TRÜFFEL IN BURGUNDER

1 *lb. truffles*	*a little chopped parsley*
¼ *pint Burgundy*	*lemon rind*

The truffles must be carefully washed so that not a particle of grit remains. Simmer in Burgundy with the chopped parsley and lemon rind until they are soft. Strain, and thicken the Burgundy with a little flour, and pour over the truffles when serving.

HEAVEN AND EARTH
HIMMEL UND ERDE
(Apples and potatoes cooked together)

1 *lb. peeled and quartered potatoes*
¼ *pint water*

1 *lb. cooking apples*
2 *oz. bacon*
salt and pepper

Cook the potatoes in boiling salted water for ten to fifteen minutes before adding the peeled, cored and quartered apples. Season with salt and pepper, and cook until soft. Dice the bacon and fry until it is crisp, and sprinkle over the apples and potatoes when serving.

This is a very typical mixture of fruit and vegetables, and is served with fried liver, kidneys or sausages.

FRICASSEE OF MUSHROOMS
CHAMPIGNONFRIKASSEE

¾ *lb. mushrooms*
2 *oz. butter*
2 *beaten egg yolks*
¼ *pint white wine*
¾ *lb. cooked meat*
3 *white rolls*
1 *oz. flour*

1 *onion*
1 *whole egg*
1 *cup milk*
juice of one lemon
salt
stock

Put the meat with the onion twice through a mincer. Soak the rolls in milk, squeeze dry, and mix with the meat. Knead well, and bind with the whole egg. Shape into balls, and poach in boiling salted water.

Lightly fry the mushrooms in butter, adding the lemon juice. Remove from the pan, and put aside, but keep hot. Add the flour to the butter to make a roux, thin with a little stock, then add the wine, and the beaten egg yolks. Stir well. Return the mushrooms to the sauce, and add the meat balls. Heat through, and sprinkle with chopped parsley.

PUMPKIN WITH CHEESE
KÜRBISBREI MIT KÄSE

2 *lb. pumpkin*	1 *oz. parmesan cheese*
1 *oz. butter*	*salt and pepper*

Peel the pumpkin, remove the seeds, and chop into pieces. Cook in salted water until soft. Strain, rub through a sieve, and mash. Season with salt and pepper, and sprinkle with parmesan cheese.

STUFFED CELERIAC
GEFÜLLTER SELLERIE

1 *large celeriac*	¼ *pint stock*
½ *lb. left-over meat*	2 *oz. white bread*
1 *teaspoon anchovy essence*	*salt and pepper*
2 *eggs*	

Peel the celeriac and cut off the top. Scoop out the

centre. Mince the meat, and mix with the bread, first soaked and squeezed dry, season with salt and pepper, and bind with the beaten eggs. Fill the scooped-out centre with the meat mixture and replace the top. Secure with a wooden cocktail stick. Bake in the oven in a casserole, with a sauce made from flour, a little white wine and lemon juice. Or braise on top of the stove, basting from time to time to prevent the celeriac from becoming dry.

CASSEROLE DISHES
AND SAVOURY PUDDINGS
ÜBERBACKENES UND AUFLÄUFE

ONION CASSEROLE
ZWIEBELAUFLAUF

1½ *lb. onions*
2 *oz. butter*
¼ *pint sour cream*
2 *egg yolks*

grated cheese
breadcrumbs
salt and pepper

Peel and thickly slice the onions. Using a casserole, simmer gently in a little butter and milk until tender. Beat the yolks, sour cream and cheese together and pour over the onions. Season.

Sprinkle liberally with cheese and breadcrumbs, and bake in a moderate oven for twenty minutes.

TOMATO
BREAD AND BUTTER PUDDING
TOMATENAUFLAUF MIT WEISSBROT

1 *lb. tomatoes*
2 *oz. butter*
About 4 thin slices of white bread
1 *tablespoon chopped parsley*
1 *teaspoon chopped chives*

1 *grated onion*
1 *beaten egg*
grated cheese
¼ *pint of sour cream*
breadcrumbs

Slice the tomatoes, butter the bread slices, and arrange

in alternate layers in a greased casserole. The top layer should be of bread. Sprinkle grated chives and onion in between the layers. Season with salt and pepper.

Mix the cream, chopped parsley and beaten egg together, and pour over the pudding. Leave for thirty minutes. Sprinkle with breadcrumbs and grated cheese, and bake for about half an hour in a moderate oven.

CAULIFLOWER WITH RICE
BLUMENKOHL MIT REIS

1 *large cauliflower*	1 *beaten egg white*
6 *oz. rice*	4 *oz. chopped bacon*
1 *oz. butter*	*breadcrumbs*
1 *oz. flour*	*chopped parsley*
2 *oz. grated cheese*	*salt and pepper*
1 *beaten egg yolk*	*paprika*

Cook the rice until soft, either in boiling water to which some meat extract has been added, or in boiling stock. Cook the cauliflower separately until tender. Just before the rice is ready, add to it the chopped bacon. Drain the cauliflower, and leave it to cool, so that it can be divided into flowerets more easily.

Strain the rice and bacon, add the beaten egg white, and put into a greased casserole. Pour in a little of the rice water, then cover with the cauliflower.

Thicken the cauliflower water with flour, add salt, paprika and chopped parsley and the beaten egg yolk. Pour this sauce over the cauliflower, sprinkle with cheese and breadcrumbs and dot with butter.

Bake in a moderate oven until brown.

SPINACH CASSEROLE

SPINATAUFLAUF

3 *lb. spinach*	¼ *pint sour cream*
1 *grated onion*	2 *oz. grated cheese*
1 *oz. butter*	*breadcrumbs*
1 *oz. flour*	*salt and pepper*
2–3 *pancakes*	1 *beaten egg*

Wash the spinach, and cook without adding water (enough will still adhere to the leaves) until it is almost tender. Make a paste with the butter and flour, and add, with the onion, to the spinach. Beat until the spinach is smooth, then put in a greased casserole. Season with salt and pepper.

Make the pancakes according to any preferred recipe, roll and arrange on the top of the spinach. Mix the sour cream with the egg and cheese, and pour over the pancakes. Sprinkle with breadcrumbs, and bake in a moderate oven until the sauce boils and the crumbs are browned.

CAULIFLOWER
WITH MUSHROOMS AND CRAB

BLUMENKOHL MIT KRABBEN UND PILZEN

1 *large cauliflower*	2 *oz. butter*
1 *small tin crab*	½ *oz. flour*
½ *lb. fresh sliced mushrooms*	1 *oz. parmesan cheese*
½ *pint milk*	*salt and pepper*

Put the cauliflower into boiling water and cook until

tender. Sauté the mushrooms in butter and season with salt and pepper. Remove the mushrooms from the pan, blend the flour with the fat, and add a little of the cauliflower water to make a sauce, then mix in the parmesan cheese. Drain the cauliflower, and when it is sufficiently cool, break into flowerets and arrange in a flat casserole. In between the flowerets arrange the crab. Pour the cheese sauce over the cauliflower and bake in a hot oven until it is browned. Garnish the top with mushrooms before serving.

If crab is not available, any strong flavoured fish will do, such as smoked bream or haddock.

SAUERKRAUT WITH POTATOES
SAUERKRAUT MIT KARTOFFELN

1 *lb. sauerkraut*	*breadcrumbs*
1 *lb. potatoes*	*grated cheese*
2 *large cooking apples*	*cooking fat*
4 *oz. bacon*	*salt*
1 *pint sour cream*	

Boil the unpeeled potatoes in salted water. Cool, peel and slice fairly thickly. Melt a little fat, and gently fry the sauerkraut, the bacon, and the apples, peeled and sliced. Arrange a layer of potatoes at the bottom of a casserole, cover with sauerkraut, bacon and apples, then add another layer of potatoes. Stir together the cream, cheese and breadcrumbs and pour over the potatoes.

Bake in a moderate oven until brown.

ASPARAGUS
SPARGEL

In Germany asparagus is used more frequently than in England, and is thinly peeled before cooking. None of it is wasted. Tough ends are used for soups and casserole dishes, and usually only the tops are served with creamed butter and brown breadcrumbs.

BAKED ASPARAGUS
SPARGEL ÜBERBACKEN

1 *lb. asparagus—ends will do*   1 *oz. grated parmesan cheese*
2 *oz. butter*   1 *oz. browned breadcrumbs*
¼ *pint Béchamel sauce*

Peel and cut the asparagus into pieces about one inch long. Cook in boiling salted water until almost tender.

Grease a casserole and arrange the asparagus in layers, pouring Béchamel sauce (see page 151) between each layer.

Sprinkle with cheese and breadcrumbs and bake in a moderate oven for thirty minutes.

ASPARAGUS WITH BACON
SPARGELAUFLAUF MIT SCHINKEN

½ *lb. asparagus*   1 *oz. butter*
1 *lb. potatoes*   1 *oz. flour*
2 *oz. grated cheese*   *breadcrumbs*
4 *oz. bacon*   *salt, pepper, ground nutmeg*
1 *egg*

Boil the potatoes in their skins, and take them from the pan before they are soft. Peel and slice. Peel and cook the asparagus in salted water until tender and cut into lengths. Arrange the potatoes, asparagus, and chopped bacon in alternate layers, the top layer being of potatoes.

Thicken with flour the liquid in which the asparagus was cooked, add the salt, pepper and nutmeg, stir and cook for three minutes. Beat the egg and quickly stir into the sauce.

Pour the sauce over the potatoes, sprinkle with cheese and breadcrumbs, dot with butter, and bake in a moderate oven until brown.

NOODLES WITH MUSHROOMS

NUDELN MIT PILZEN

½ lb. wide noodles
½ lb. mushrooms
1 large onion
3 oz. grated cheese

1 whole egg
breadcrumbs
salt and pepper
1 oz. butter

Cook the noodles in boiling salted water for ten minutes. Strain and put into a greased casserole. Slice the mushrooms and the onion, and sauté in butter until tender. Add to the noodles. Mix in most of the cheese, reserving some for sprinkling over the top.

Beat the egg, and stir into the mushroom fat, adding a little boiling water to make a sauce. Pour the sauce over the noodles and mushrooms. Sprinkle with cheese and breadcrumbs and dot with small nobs of butter.

Bake in a moderate oven for twenty to twenty-five minutes.

FISH, BACON AND POTATO PIE

FISCHSCHÜSSEL

2 *lb. fish*	*fish stock*
1 *lb. potatoes*	1 *cup of meat gravy*
4 *oz. streaky bacon*	

Clean the fish and cook in stock until tender. Skin, bone and cut into large pieces. Boil the potatoes in their skins, peel and slice. Arrange the fish and potatoes in layers in a well-greased casserole. Between each layer put pieces of bacon, and moisten with gravy.

Bake in a very hot oven for about fifteen minutes and serve with a lettuce or cucumber salad.

MUSHROOM PUDDING

PILZPUDDING

German pudding basins have fitted lids and are usually made of aluminium. In the middle there is a cone, which gives a deep hollow to the pudding when it is turned out. This is useful for filling with sauces or fruit.

1 *lb. mushrooms*	3 *beaten egg whites*
2 *oz. butter*	3 *tablespoons cream*
1 *chopped onion*	1 *tablespoon chopped parsley*
6 *tablespoons breadcrumbs*	*salt*
3 *beaten egg yolks*	

Wash and slice the mushrooms, and fry with the onions in butter for ten minutes. Add the breadcrumbs and fry for one minute longer. Remove the pan from the stove, stir in the beaten egg yolks and cream, add the salt and parsley, and finally the egg whites. Pour into a pudding basin and steam for one hour.

Serve with a mushroom sauce.

POTATO CHEESE PUDDING
KARTOFFEL-KÄSEPUDDING

1 *lb. cooked and riced potatoes*	2 *tablespoons milk*
3 *oz. butter*	4–5 *oz. grated cheese*
3 *egg yolks*	*salt and paprika pepper*
3 *beaten egg whites*	

Cream the butter and egg yolks together, add the potatoes, seasonings, cheese and milk. Beat well, and then fold in the egg whites. Half fill a pudding basin, cover tightly, and steam for one hour. Leave for fifteen minutes in the basin before turning out.

Serve with a hot tomato sauce and surrounded by mixed vegetables.

BACON AND POTATO PUDDING
SCHINKEN-KARTOFFEL PUDDING

2 *lb. cooked potatoes*	1 *tablespoon chopped parsley*
3 *oz. stale bread*	1 *tablespoon chopped chives*
½ *lb. chopped bacon*	1 *chopped onion*
2 *eggs*	*salt and paprika pepper*
1 *tablespoon butter*	

Put the potatoes and the bacon together twice through a mincer, the second time adding the bread, previously soaked and squeezed dry. Sauté the onion, beat the eggs, and with the parsley, chives, salt and paprika, add to the potatoes and bacon. Mix well and turn into a well-greased pudding basin and steam for thirty to forty minutes.

Turn out, and serve surrounded by mixed vegetables and with a savoury sauce.

BURIED HAM

SCHINKENBEGRÄBNIS

(Ham and cheese macaroni)

¾ lb. macaroni	2 oz. grated cheese
½ lb. ham	¼ pint sour cream
2 egg yolks	salt and pepper

Bring some salted water to the boil and gently add the macaroni. Cook until tender, that is about ten to fifteen minutes. Strain and while still in the sieve pass quickly under cold running water. Chop the ham into small pieces, then put with the macaroni in a casserole. Season with salt and pepper. Beat the eggs and the cream together, and pour over the macaroni. Sprinkle with cheese, and bake in a moderate oven until the sauce has cooked and become a light brown.

Gammon bacon may be used instead of ham.

DUMPLINGS
KLÖSSE

POTATO DUMPLINGS
KARTOFFELKLÖSSE

1 *lb. cooked potatoes*	2 *oz. potato flour*
1 *beaten egg*	3 *slices bread*
2 *oz. flour*	*salt and pepper*

The potatoes should be cooked the previous day, as freshly cooked potatoes are inclined to come apart when being re-cooked.

Press the potatoes through a ricer, then mix to a dough, with the salt, pepper, flour, potato flour and egg. Dice the bread and fry in butter until crisp. Put the potato dough on to a floured board and shape into a long baton-like roll. Cut into pieces of equal size and press a piece of the diced bread into each. Shape into dumplings, and drop into boiling salted water. Cook for ten to fifteen minutes. Drain and serve immediately with melted butter.

PLUM POTATO DUMPLINGS
ZWETSCHGENKNÖDEL

These are made in the same way as Potato Dumplings, except that the bread is omitted and a stoned plum, with a knob of sugar in its centre, is used instead. When serving, sprinkle with fried breadcrumbs.

COTTAGE CHEESE PLUM DUMPLINGS
ZWETSCHGENKNÖDEL AUS TOPFENTEIG

½ lb. cottage cheese   2 oz. soft breadcrumbs
½ lb. plums (small)   ½ oz. butter
2 eggs   salt and pepper
4 oz. flour

Mix the cheese (which should be very dry) with the eggs, butter, salt, pepper and flour to a firm dough. Leave in a cool place for forty-five minutes.

Meanwhile stone the plums and in the centre of each place a lump of sugar. Break off pieces of the dough, put a sugar-plum in the middle of each piece, and shape into a dumpling. Drop into boiling water and cook for ten minutes. Drain and sprinkle with fried breadcrumbs when serving.

NAPKIN DUMPLING WITH PEARS AND BEANS
SERVIETTENKLÖSSE MIT BIRNEN UND BOHNEN

DUMPLING:

6 oz. diced white bread   3 eggs
1 oz. melted butter   ½ cup milk

Fry the bread in butter. Beat the eggs and milk together and pour over the bread. Leave until the bread is soft. Mix into a paste. Grease a white napkin with butter, and put the bread in the middle. Gather up the ends of the cloth and tie tightly, leaving a little space for the dumpling to swell. Put into a pan of boiling water and cook for thirty minutes.

PEARS AND BEANS :

2 *lb. cooking pears*   3 *rashers diced fat bacon*
strip of lemon rind   2 *tablespoons vinegar*
2 *lb. French beans*   *juice of half a lemon*
2 *oz. sugar*   *pepper*

Peel and slice the pears, and cook in boiling water for fifteen minutes. Add the beans, trimmed and broken into halves, and the lemon rind. Fry the bacon until crisp but not burnt. Take from the pan and keep warm. Add the sugar to the bacon fat, then the lemon juice, vinegar and pepper. Stir well, and add a little of the water in which the pears are cooking. Simmer for three minutes. Pour this sauce over the still cooking pears and beans, and continue simmering until both are tender. Strain. By this time, the dumpling is ready to be turned out on to a plate. Surround with the pears and beans, and garnish with the diced bacon.

DUMPLINGS (SWEET)
DAMPFKNÖDEL

½ *oz. baker's yeast*   2 *eggs*
½ *lb. flour*   ¼ *pint milk*
2 *oz. butter*   *vanilla essence*
1 *oz. sugar*

Dissolve the yeast in warm milk. Cream the butter, sugar and eggs together. Add the flour, then the yeast, and knead until the dough begins to blister and come away from the bowl. Leave to rise in a warm place until it doubles its size. Roll out the dough, and shape into balls. Leave once more to rise. Grease a roasting pan with butter, then add the milk, flavoured with vanilla.

Lay the dumplings in the tin, cover first with a cloth, then a lid and cook on top of the stove for thirty minutes. As the milk begins to steam the fat will crackle, and the dumplings will rise and become a golden brown. Serve with stewed fruit.

APPLE DUMPLINGS

APFELKLOESSE

1 *lb. apples*	4 *oz. soft breadcrumbs*
1 *oz. sweet almonds*	½ *pint milk*
rind of half a lemon	2 *oz. butter*
4 *oz. currants*	4 *eggs*
3 *oz. sugar*	*brown sugar*
pinch of ground cinnamon	

Peel and cut the apples into small pieces. Blanch and grind the almonds. Melt the butter, beat the eggs until frothy and then mix all the ingredients together. If the mixture does not appear sufficiently stiff to make firm dumplings add some more breadcrumbs. Form the mixture into small, round balls and drop them into boiling and slightly salted water. They will take about 15 minutes to cook. Serve with browned butter still hot from the pan and sprinkle with brown sugar mixed with ground cinnamon.

FRIED DUMPLINGS

GEBRATENE KNÖDEL

½ *lb. flour*	4 *eggs*
¼ *pint cream*	½ *oz. baker's yeast*
¼ *pint milk*	*sugar and salt to taste*
2 *oz. melted butter*	

Dissolve the yeast in warm milk. Sieve the flour and make a hollow in the centre. Drop in one whole egg and three egg yolks, the cream, the melted butter, sugar, salt and yeast. Work into a dough and knead until it blisters and comes away from the bowl. Lightly sprinkle with flour, cover with a cloth and leave in a warm place until it rises twice its size. Break off pieces and shape into rings, with a hole in the middle large enough to slip in half a crown. Fry the dumplings in a covered pan in deep fat till the underside is brown. Turn, and brown the other side, this time leaving the pan uncovered. Drain on absorbent paper, sprinkle with sugar and serve.

These dumplings can also be fried in butter until they are crisp, but not brown, and served with soup— or flatten the dumpling and fill with creamed spinach, double over, dampen the edges with beaten egg, and pinch together tightly. Drop into boiling water, cover, and cook for about twenty minutes. Drain and serve with melted butter and parmesan cheese.

BREAD DUMPLINGS
SEMMELKLÖSSE

8 *white rolls*
1 *oz. sugar*
1 *oz. chopped almonds*

1 *oz. stoned raisins*
2 *beaten egg yolks*
2 *beaten egg whites*

Soak the rolls in milk until they swell, then squeeze them out in a cloth. Mix the bread, sugar, almonds, raisins and egg yolks to a paste. Finally fold in the beaten egg whites. Shape into small balls, and fry in deep boiling fat. Try one first, if it does not hold, then add some breadcrumbs to the mixture.

Stoned and cooked prunes can be used instead of almonds and raisins.

BREAD DUMPLINGS (BOILED)
SEMMELKLÖSSE (GEKOCHT)

½ *lb. stale French bread*   3 *beaten egg whites*
1 *oz. melted butter*   1 *oz. flour*
3 *egg yolks*   *salt*

Soak the bread and squeeze in a cloth. Mix it to a paste with the egg yolks, salt, melted butter and flour. Finally fold in the egg whites. Shape into balls, and boil for either fifteen minutes in boiling salted water, or for thirty minutes with stewed fruit, allowing plenty of water for cooking.

SEMOLINA DUMPLINGS
GRIESSKLÖSSCHEN

1 *pint milk and water mixed*   3 *oz. semolina*
½ *oz. butter*   2 *eggs*
¼ *teaspoon sugar*   *salt*

Bring the milk and water with the butter, sugar and salt, to the boil. Throw in the semolina, and stir over a very low heat until the mixture comes away cleanly from the bottom of the saucepan. Leave the semolina to cool a little, then beat in one egg. When this is thoroughly mixed, add the second egg.

Break off small pieces, shape into balls, poach in boiling water, and serve with sweet soups.

FISH DUMPLINGS
FISCHKLÖSSE

½ lb. boned raw fish
1 white roll (soaked and squeezed dry)
¼ pint stock or milk
1 oz. butter

1 small grated onion
1 egg yolk
teaspoon of chopped parsley
½ oz. grated parmesan cheese
salt and pepper

Put the fish through a mincing machine. Melt the butter, add the onion and bread and lightly fry. Mix with the other ingredients into a firm mass. Break off pieces and shape into large dumplings. Roll in flour and cook in boiling salted water. Handle the dumplings with care, otherwise they may come apart.

Serve with mashed potatoes and a well-seasoned white sauce.

LIVER DUMPLINGS (Bavarian)
LEBERKNÖDEL

8 white rolls
½ pint milk
½ lb. chopped liver
butter
2 beaten eggs

1 small chopped onion
chopped parsley
1 clove garlic
salt

Slice the rolls and soak in milk in a covered bowl. Squeeze dry. Fry lightly the chopped onion, garlic and parsley in the smallest possible amount of butter, then add to the bread, with the beaten eggs and liver. Knead to a paste. Break off pieces and shape into dumplings, and lay them side by side in a large saucepan. Pour in salted boiling water to cover, and cook for twenty minutes.

Serve with boiled cabbage and an onion sauce.

SNOW DUMPLINGS FOR FRUIT SOUPS
SCHNEEKLÖSSCHEN FÜR SUPPEN

2 *egg whites*   2 *oz. castor sugar*

Beat the egg whites stiffly, then fold in the sugar. Pour the mixture into a pan filled with boiling water, cover, and then draw the pan to the side of the stove. Leave for fifteen minutes. When the mixture has swollen, divide with a knife into small dumplings, remove with a draining spoon, and serve at once.

MEAT DUMPLINGS
FLEISCHKLÖSSCHEN

4 *oz. cooked meat*   1 *teaspoon butter*
1 *large boiled potato*   1 *teaspoon chopped onion*
1 *beaten egg white*   *salt and paprika pepper*

Put the meat and potato through a mincer. Fry the onion in the butter, and mix with the meat, egg white, salt and paprika pepper. Knead into a firm paste.

Break off small pieces, shape into balls and poach either in boiling water or in hot soup. Do not overcook.

COTTAGE CHEESE DUMPLINGS
QUARKKLÖSSE

12 oz. cottage cheese
3 oz. butter
3 whole eggs

4 tablespoons soft breadcrumbs
grated rind of half a lemon
1 oz. sugar

Beat the butter to a cream then add the rest of the ingredients, dropping in each egg separately.

Break off pieces, shape into dumplings, and cook in boiling water for ten minutes.

Serve with melted butter, or with a vanilla sauce.

POTATO SALAD
KARTOFFELSALAT

Boil the potatoes in their skins, and while still warm peel, and slice and put into a large bowl. Pour the following dressing over the still warm potatoes.

Mix together one tablespoon of salad oil to four tablespoons of vinegar. Add some finely chopped onion, a little diced bacon, and season. Put into a pan, bring to the boil, and use immediately.

In Bavaria they add three or four tablespoons of hot stock to the dressing.

If a cold dressing is preferred, add one well beaten egg to the ingredients, omit the bacon and do not boil.

Mixed dried or fresh herbs, chopped green olives and anchovies are often added to the salad.

POTATO SALAD
WITH SAUCE PIQUANT
KARTOFFELSALAT MIT PIKANTER SAUCE

1 *lb. cooked potatoes*	1 *teaspoon dried mustard*
2 *egg yolks*	4 *chopped shallots*
4 *tablespoons olive oil*	1 *tablespoon capers*
1 *tablespoon tarragon vinegar*	4 *tablespoons meat stock*
1 *glass red wine*	

Stir the oil, vinegar, red wine, stock and mustard together, adding the shallots and capers. Beat the egg yolks into the dressing until it is thick. Slice the still warm potatoes, sprinkle with salt and pour the dressing over them.

When making potato salad with mayonnaise, add some yoghourt or sour cream as the Bavarians do. Rub the bowl with garlic and add a little crisp, tart diced apple.

CHICORY SALAD
ZICHORIENSALAT

½ lb. chicory   *pepper and salt*
3 tablespoons salad oil 1 tablespoon vinegar

Remove the bruised outer leaves. Pull the chicory apart and wash in lemon flavoured water to prevent discoloration. Chop finely. Pour over a dressing of mixed salad oil and vinegar.

Cooked green peas and chopped onion are pleasant additions to this salad.

BEETROOT SALAD
ROTE-RÜBEN-SALAT

1. Dice cooked beetroot while still warm and lay in a marinade of vinegar, sliced onions, carraway seeds and peppercorns. Next day, dry the beetroots and pour over them a dressing made from sour cream, mustard and grated onion. Add a pinch of sugar.

2. Pour a French dressing over some sliced beetroots and sprinkle with salt.

3. Slice the beetroots and lay in vinegar, sprinkle with salt and carraway seeds. Serve chilled.

LETTUCE SALAD WITH BACON
KOPFSALAT MIT SPECK

Wash the lettuce and separate the leaves. Arrange on a salad dish. Fry about two ounces of diced bacon in olive oil until it is crisp. Add a little brown sugar and enough vinegar to make a dressing. Pour the hot dressing over the lettuce, and serve while the lettuce is still warm from the dressing.

CHEESE SALAD
KÄSESALAT

Finely chop some strongly flavoured cheese and sprinkle with carraway seeds. Moisten with a vinaigrette sauce, and serve with white wine. This is generally considered a man's dish.

HERRING SALAD
HERINGSSALAT

10 *cooked peeled potatoes*	1 *gherkin*
3 *peeled raw apples*	1–2 *slices cold meat*
2 *salted filleted herrings*	1 *onion*
with roes	*salad oil*

Chop all the ingredients into small pieces, sprinkle with salt, and mix with two tablespoons of salad oil. Mash the herring roes and mix with two tablespoons of wine vinegar, a teaspoon of dried mustard, and the same amount of sugar. Pour this dressing over the herring salad, arrange in a salad dish, surrounded with sliced gherkin, capers and chopped hard-boiled egg.

If salted herrings are not available, rollmops can be substituted.

GHERKIN SALAD

GURKENSALAT

Slice some pickled cucumber and cover with a French dressing, salt and pepper. Peasants along the Polish border add thick slices of cooked potatoes and cold sliced beetroot. Smother in sour cream.

MEAT SALAD

FLEISCHSALAT

Cooked potatoes, raw celery, raw carrots, apples and cheese, all chopped, form the basis of this salad. Add chopped cold meat, mix with mayonnaise, sliced gherkins, chopped parsley and tomatoes.

FISH SALAD

FISCHSALAT

Cooked pike, carp, salmon or lobster can be used for this salad. Cut the fish into small pieces and roll in mayonnaise. Arrange in a salad bowl and garnish with hard-boiled eggs, capers and sliced gherkins. If available, strips of rolled smoked salmon and shrimps can be used as a garnish.

Serve with watercress, green salad or plain lettuce.

PEASANT SALAD

BAUERNSALAT

Shredded white and red cabbage, combined with lettuce and watercress, are used for this simple salad.

Mix some mayonnaise and sour cream together, and pour over the salad. Garnish with sliced tomatoes and gherkins.

WHITE BEAN SALAD

WEISSE-BOHNEN-SALAT

Soak overnight some haricot or butter beans, and cook next day in salted water until tender. While still warm, mix with a little olive oil, chopped onion, sliced gherkin and chopped capers. Chill before serving.

FRENCH BEAN SALAD

GRÜNE-BOHNEN-SALAT

Tie some young French beans into bundles and cook in salted water. Untie the bundles, drain, and leave to get cold. Mix with a little olive oil and thinly-sliced onion. Add some diced gherkins and chopped capers.

SPINACH SALAD

SPINATSALAT

1 *lb. spinach*	1 *teaspoon vinegar*
3 *tablespoons oil*	*salt*

Wash in salted water some very young spinach and cook until tender in just enough water to cover the bottom of the pan. Rinse quickly in cold water, drain, and using a wooden spoon mix with the oil and vinegar.

CUCUMBER SALAD WITH CREAM
GURKENSALAT MIT SAHNE

1 *cucumber*
4 *tablespoons sour cream*
1 *tablespoon vinegar*

salt, pepper
chives, dill and borage (chopped)

Peel and slice the cucumber, mix with the cream and the other ingredients.

If available, add chopped hard-boiled egg yolk.

QUEEN'S SALAD
KÖNIGIN-SALAT

Pour about five tablespoons of salad cream or mayonnaise into a small round dish. Place in the middle a scooped-out artichoke bottom, filled with meat salad.

Surround with half slices of tomato, and garnish with small sprigs of parsley.

CHICORY PLATE
ZICHORIENSALAT

Arrange two or three sticks of chopped celeriac on a plate, and spread with mayonnaise. Cover with a layer of raw chicory, spread another layer of mayonnaise and then a layer of thinly-sliced stewed pears.

The pears should be stewed in a little red wine.

BRUNSWICK CASTLE SALAD
BRAUNSCHWEIGER SCHLOSS SALAT

1 *lb. celeriac*	*About two tablespoons*
4 *oz. truffles*	*mayonnaise*
1 *tablespoon oil*	2 *hard-boiled eggs*
½ *tablespoon vinegar*	*tarragon*

Cook the celeriac and slice thinly. Lay with the truffles (the tinned variety is used for this salad) in oil and vinegar. Add the mayonnaise and some chopped fresh tarragon. Leave until required and garnish with slices of hard-boiled egg.

If celeriac is not available, use celery.

SAUERKRAUT SALAD
SAUERKRAUTSALAT

¾ *lb. sauerkraut*	1 *grated apple*
4 *tablespoons olive oil*	*pepper*

Stir all the ingredients together with a wooden spoon—neither salt nor vinegar is necessary.

SANDWICHES
BELEGTE BRÖTE

Open sandwiches are an important feature in German menus. The really imaginative housewife can produce an amazing variety and has in any case an almost exhaustive store from which to choose. For example there are a dozen or more different types of liver sausage, tea sausage or Mettwurst, and each district has its own speciality. Again there is tremendous choice to be found on the cold meat counter of the delicatessen shops, smoked bacon, ham, cold roast pork or beef, etc.

Therefore it follows that there is no end to the variations of the open sandwich. I have given only a few, to try and offer some idea of what they can be. Rye bread is almost always used, and the bread is cut into slices of medium thickness.

HAM OR BACON SANDWICH
SCHINKEN BRÖTE

Spread slices of rye bread with butter. Completely cover with thin slices of smoked bacon or ham, and garnish with chopped gherkin.

LIVER SAUSAGE SANDWICH
LEBERWURST BRÖTE

Spread some slices of rye bread thinly with butter, and then with liver sausage. To add to their appearance the slices can be cut into triangles and each garnished with chopped gherkins.

SAVOURY SANDWICH
DELICATTESSEN BRÖTE

Spread slices of toast with butter, sprinkle with curry powder then spread thinly with sour cream. Add capers, chopped hard boiled egg, sliced tomatoes and gherkins.

SAILOR'S SANDWICH
MATROSEN-BRÖTE

Rub some hard-boiled eggs through a sieve, then mix with parsley butter, salt, lemon juice and a little dry mustard. Spread on slices of rye bread, and garnish with fillets of anchovy and chopped gherkins.

TARTAR SANDWICH
TARTAREN-BRÖTE

Put some fresh raw meat through a mincer with enough chopped onion to flavour it. Spread a layer of the raw minced meat on some buttered rye bread. Make a hollow in the centre of the meat, season with salt and pepper, and in the middle drop one raw egg yolk. Sprinkle on a little grated horseradish.

SARDINE SANDWICH
SARDINEN-BRÖTE

Spread some slices of rye bread with anchovy butter, and on each slice arrange one large filleted sardine.

Sprinkle with lemon juice and add a few capers for decoration.

GARLIC BREAD
KNOBLAUCHBROT

1 *rye loaf*   *garlic*   *butter*

Slice the loaf lengthwise. Spread each slice with butter and pounded garlic. Put the slices back as they were, and press down with a heavy weight. Serve cold, or put the loaf into a tin and warm through in the oven. White bread may also be used in this way. It is usual to serve garlic bread with strong black coffee.

EGG AND CREAM SANDWICH
EIERMITSAHNE-BRÖTE

Spread some rye bread with butter. Mash the yolks of two or three hard-boiled eggs, and spread over the bread. Thinly cover with sour cream, and garnish with sliced tomato and chopped gherkin.

PUMPERNICKEL
PUMPERNICKEL

Pumpernickel is a type of black bread and a speciality of Westphalia. It is usually sold sliced in square or round packets. Its peculiar name is said to be derived from the remark of a Frenchman who, during the

Napoleonic wars, ate some pumpernickel and declared
that it was '*bon pour le nickel*'. A nickel is a small coin.

PUMPERNICKEL SANDWICH
PUMPERNICKEL SCHNITTEN

Spread six or seven slices of pumpernickel thinly with
butter and cream cheese. Place one on top of the other,
adding one plain slice on the top. Cut through, and
serve in portions about one inch square.

Another form of pumpernickel sandwich is to cut
through the centre of a crusty roll, spread with butter,
and then put a slice of pumpernickel between the two
halves. This is called the 'black and white' special.

COTTAGE CHEESE
QUARK

COTTAGE cheese is used far more in Germany than in
England, especially in cakes, dumplings and spreads.
The latter are good for open sandwiches. Here are just
a few of the many variations you will find all over
Germany.

PARSLEY CHEESE
KRÄUTERKÄSE

To half a pound of cheese add two heaped tablespoons
of finely chopped parsley. Flavour with a little sugar
and beat in half a gill of cream.

Chopped dill, chopped chives or other similar herbs may be used instead of parsley.

CARRAWAY CHEESE

KÜMMELKÄSE

Mix about one teaspoon of carraway seeds with half a pound of cheese, then beat in half a gill of fresh cream.

ANCHOVY CHEESE

SARDELLEN-KÄSE

Mix as above, using chopped and filleted anchovies. Cold chopped meat can also be used, as well as finely diced carrots.

PEASANT CAVIAR

BAUERN-CAVIAR

Beat half a pound of cottage cheese with four ounces of grated Edamer cheese, one small grated onion, and half a teaspoon of paprika pepper.

PARSLEY BUTTER

KRÄUTERBUTTER

Cream two ounces of butter with a dessertspoon of lemon juice, one tablespoon of chopped parsley, and chopped chives to taste.

ANCHOVY BUTTER
SARDELLENBUTTER

Cream two ounces of butter with about one ounce of anchovies, previously rubbed through a sieve.

COTTAGE CHEESE WITH BEER
QUARK MIT BIER

Beat half a pound of cottage cheese with enough beer to thin it slightly; about two tablespoons should be enough. Add one small chopped onion, and half a teaspoon of paprika.

COLD BEEF SANDWICH
RINDFLEISCH-BRÖTE

Arrange some thin slices of underdone cold beef on buttered rye bread. Garnish with chopped gherkins and small pieces of jellied consommé, and sprinkle with grated horseradish.

CHEESE SANDWICH
KÄSE-BRÖTE

Spread slices of rye bread with parsley butter, then fairly thickly with cream cheese. Sprinkle with carraway seeds.

TEA SAUSAGE SANDWICH
METTWURST-BRÖTE

Slice some Mettwurst very thinly and spread on slices of rye bread, which have been spread with parsley butter. Garnish with slices of tomato and gherkin.

SNIPE AND LIVER SANDWICH
SCHNEPFENBROETCHEN

intestines of one snipe
1 oz. goose liver
4 chopped small mushrooms
1 teaspoon chopped fresh
  parsley
12 capers
½ oz. soft breadcrumbs
1 boned sardine

1 shallot
½ oz. butter
½ oz. Parmesan cheese
lemon juice
½ egg yolk
salt and pepper
1 slice of fried bread

Finely chop the intestines with the liver. Mix both with mushrooms, parsley, capers, breadcrumbs, sardine, shallot, salt and pepper. Heat the butter and lightly steam the mixed ingredients. Push the mixture through a fine wire sieve. Add the egg yolk. Have ready a thick slice of bread fried in butter. Pile the mixture onto this and sprinkle with the cheese, finely grated. Add two or three thin slivers of butter, flavour with a few drops of lemon juice and bake for a few minutes in a moderate oven before serving.

WHITE ROUX
WEISSE EINBRENNE

1 *oz. butter*   1 *oz. flour*

Melt the butter in a pan, blend in the flour and cook over a low fire for two minutes, stirring all the time.

BROWN ROUX
BRAUNE EINBRENNE

1 *oz. butter*   1 *oz. flour*

The same as for white roux, but cook until golden brown.

WHITE SAUCE
WEISSESAUCE

1 *oz. butter*   ¼ *pint white stock*
1 *oz. flour*   *bayleaves*
½ *pint milk*   *salt and pepper*

Melt the butter, blend in the flour, and cook for a few minutes without browning. Thin with milk, stirring all the time, and bring once to the boil. Add the stock and bayleaves and simmer for another ten minutes. Remove bayleaves, and season to taste

This sauce forms the basis for many other sauces, and can be used alone.

Although these sauces are by no means all strictly German, they are included because they are often mentioned in the recipes. I have given, however, the German way of making them, even for such well-known sauces as Béchamel.

BÉCHAMEL SAUCE
BÉCHAMELSAUCE

1 *oz. lean bacon*	½ *oz. flour*
2 *oz. sliced onion*	¼ *pint meat stock*
1 *oz. butter*	¼ *pint cream*

Melt the butter, and fry the onion and diced bacon. Stir in the flour, cook for a few minutes, then gradually add the stock and the cream. Simmer until the sauce is smooth, strain and serve hot.

CHEESE SAUCE
KÄSESAUCE

1 *tablespoon basic white roux*	½ *teaspoon lemon juice*
¼ *pint sour cream*	*salt and paprika pepper*
4 *tablespoons grated cheese*	¼ *pint water*

Thin the roux with the water, and cook until smooth, stirring all the time. Add the cream, salt and pepper. Remove from the fire, then beat in the lemon juice, and the grated cheese. Serve hot.

This sauce is especially good with vegetables, fish, or hard-boiled eggs.

FROTHY WINE SAUCE

WEINSCHAUMSAUCE

2 whole eggs
2 egg yolks
2 tablespoons lemon juice

2 oz. sugar
1 teaspoon lemon sugar
¼ pint white wine

Beat all the ingredients together in a basin. Put the basin over a pan of boiling water and continue beating until the sauce boils. Put the sauce aside. If it should separate and not remain thick, it must be returned to the basin and the beating renewed. The best way is to test some of the sauce in a glass. If it remains firm then the sauce is ready.

HORSERADISH SAUCE

MEERRETTISCHSAUCE

1 oz. butter
1 oz. flour
¼ pint water
¼ pint milk

salt
2 tablespoons grated horse-
　radish
sugar to taste

Prepare a basic white sauce from the flour, butter, milk and water, and when it is smooth, add the horseradish, salt and sugar. Mix well, and serve very hot.

KUMMEL SAUCE
KÜMMELSAUCE

Make a smooth white roux, thin with a meat stock, and two tablespoons of white wine. Add carraway seeds to taste. Flavour with salt, pepper and a little lemon juice.

LEMON SAUCE
ZITRONENSAUCE

½ *pint milk*	¼ *oz. potato flour*
½ *oz. sugar*	*rind of half a lemon*
2 *egg yolks*	*pinch of salt*

Beat the egg yolks with the milk, then put into the top of a double boiler and bring to the boil, adding the lemon rind, sugar and salt.

Thicken with potato flour, or cornflour. Strain, and serve hot.

MADEIRA SAUCE
MADEIRASAUCE

1 *oz. butter*	¼ *pint Madeira*
1 *oz. chopped onion*	*mixed dried herbs*
½ *oz. flour*	*sugar and pepper*
¼ *pint brown gravy*	

Fry the onion in the butter, add the flour, and cook

until both are browned. Add the rest of the ingredients, stir until smooth, then strain through a sieve. Return to the pan, reheat slowly, add two or three tablespoons more of madeira, and a knob of butter. Stir until the butter has melted, and serve hot.

A Burgundy sauce is made in the same way, substituting Burgundy for madeira.

MIXED HERB SAUCE
KRÄUTERSAUCE

1 tablespoon basic white roux
¼ pint sour cream
1 teaspoon chopped chives
1 teaspoon chopped basil
1½ teaspoons chopped sage
salt and pepper
¼ pint water

Thin the roux with the water and the sour cream. When the mixture is quite smooth, and the flour quite cooked, remove from the heat, season with salt and pepper, and quickly beat in the chopped herbs. Serve hot.

MUSHROOM SAUCE
CHAMPIGNONSAUCE

½ lb. peeled mushrooms
½ oz. butter
½ oz. flour
mixed dried herbs
½ pint brown meat stock
1 teaspoon lemon juice
1 tablespoon madeira
pinch of salt and sugar

Slice the mushrooms and lightly fry in melted butter.
Take out the mushrooms, and put aside, but keep hot.
Stir the flour into the mushroom butter, and brown.
Gradually add the stock, salt and sugar, lemon juice,
and herbs.

Stir altogether and cook for a few minutes. Return
the mushrooms to the sauce, and after cooking them for
a few more minutes, add the wine, stir and serve while
still hot.

REMOULADE SAUCE

REMOULADENSAUCE

½ oz. olive oil	1 teaspoon German mustard
½ oz. flour	½ teaspoon sugar
¼ pint stock	a little fresh tarragon, chives
1 beaten egg yolk	and parsley
1 hard-boiled yolk (mashed)	

Blanch the herbs in boiling water for a few moments,
then chop very finely. Make a white roux from the oil
and flour, then gradually add the stock until the sauce
is thick and smooth. Add mustard, chopped herbs, egg
yolks, (both raw and cooked), and sugar. Simmer for a
few minutes, stirring all the time, then rub through
a very fine sieve. Season the sieved sauce with salt
and pepper, and thin if necessary with a little wine
vinegar.

TOMATO SAUCE
TOMATENSAUCE

1 *lb. tomatoes*	¼ *pint meat stock*
1 *oz. butter*	1 *beaten egg yolk*
1 *oz. flour*	1 *teaspoon lemon juice*
1 *oz. raw diced bacon*	*mixed dried herbs*
½ *oz. chopped onion*	*salt and sugar to taste*

Melt the butter in a pan, add the bacon and onion and fry together. Stir in the flour and cook for three minutes. Gradually add the stock, and when this is boiling add the tomatoes, chopped but not peeled. Simmer until they are tender, then rub through a sieve. Return to the pan, add the herbs, sugar, seasonings and beaten egg yolk. Serve hot.

TRUFFLE SAUCE
TRÜFFELSAUCE

1 *oz. flour*	½ *oz. tinned truffles*
1 *oz. butter*	¼ *pint madeira*
½ *chopped onion*	¼ *pint red wine*
¼ *pint brown gravy*	*mixed herbs*

From the butter and flour make a brown roux, then add the onion, and gradually the gravy and madeira. Add the herbs and the truffle, and cook, stirring all the time, until the sauce is smooth. Strain through a sieve, then flavour with the red wine. Stir in a small knob of butter, and serve hot.

FRICASEE SAUCE

FRIKASEESAUCE

This is made in precisely the same way as the above sauce, omitting the truffle, and seasoning with cayenne pepper. A little lemon juice may also be added.

BASIC SEMOLINA FLUMMERY RECIPE
FLAMMERI

4 *oz. semolina*   3 *oz. sugar*
1 *pint milk*   2 *beaten egg whites*
2 *tablespoons sultanas*

Bring the milk to the boil before throwing in the semolina. Cook for a full fiftee minutes, stirring all the while. Add sugar and sultanas. When the semolina is thick, remove from the fire, beat well, then fold in the egg whites. Pour into a rinsed mould and leave to set. Serve cold.

LEMON FLUMMERY
ZITRONENFLAMMERI

Use the basic recipe, omitting sultanas and eggs, and substituting the juice of two lemons and the grated rind of one lemon.

CHOCOLATE FLUMMERY
SCHOKOLADENFLAMMERI

Use basic recipe, omitting sultanas, and adding three ounces of grated chocolate to the semolina after ten minutes' cooking.

FRESH FRUIT FLUMMERY
FRISCHE OBST FLAMMERI

Use basic recipe, omitting sultanas, and substituting soft fruits, such as crushed strawberries, or raspberries, cooked sieved rhubarb or apple purée.

SAGO

Sago is cooked in exactly the same way as semolina. Sometimes red wine is used with sago, instead of milk, and a little more sugar is then added.

FARINA PUDDING
GRIESSPUDDING

½ *pint milk*	1 *teaspoon grated lemon rind*
2 *oz. butter*	1 *oz. ground almonds*
4 *oz. farina (potato flour)*	3 *beaten egg whites*
salt	3 *egg yolks*
3 *oz. sugar*	

Bring the milk with the butter to the boil, then throw in the farina. Cook on a very low heat until it swells, then take quickly from the heat and beat in one egg yolk. Leave to cool.

Gradually beat in the other egg yolks, the almonds, sugar, and lemon rind, and finally when the mixture is sufficiently smooth, add the egg whites.

Pour the mixture into a pudding form, cover to prevent a crust forming and chill. Unmould and serve with stewed fruit.

VANILLA CREAM JELLY
VANILLECREME

1 *pint milk*	½ *pint whipped cream*
4 *egg yolks*	1 *oz. gelatine*
3 *oz. sugar*	*vanilla flavouring*

Scald the milk, and gradually pour it over the egg yolks previously creamed together with the sugar. Cook in a double boiler until the mixture thickens, then add the flavouring and the gelatine, first dissolved in water. Beat the mixture until it cools, then add the whipped cream. Pour into a rinsed mould and leave to set.

ORANGE CREAM JELLY
ORANGENCREME

4 *egg yolks*	*juice of six oranges and two*
4 *oz. sugar*	*lemons*
½ *pint white wine*	1 *cup whipped cream*
1 *oz. gelatine*	

Dissolve the gelatine. Heat the wine, add the eggs and sugar (previously beaten together). Continue cooking in a double boiler until the mixture thickens. Remove from the fire, and quickly add the gelatine and the orange and lemon juice.

If there is not at least half a pint of juice, add a little more wine.

Strain, and pour into a bowl. As the mixture begins to thicken whisk in the cream. Pour into a rinsed mould, and leave to set. Turn out, and garnish with slices of preserved orange.

COFFEE CREAM
KAFFEECREME

½ *pint vanilla cream jelly* ¼ *pint strong black coffee*
 (*see previous page*) 1 *tablespoon of Kirsch*

Stir the coffee and Kirsch into the vanilla cream, after the gelatine has been added.

CHESTNUT CREAM
KASTANIENCREME

½ *pint vanilla cream jelly* 5 *oz. chestnut purée*
 (*see previous page*) 3 *tablespoons rum*

Roast the chestnuts until it is possible to remove the outer shell and the inner brown skin. Cook in water until soft, drain and rub through a sieve. Add to the vanilla cream after the gelatine, then add the rum.

BOILED RICE WITH APPLES
APFELREIS

8 *oz. rice*   2 *oz. sultanas*
1 *quart boiling water* *vanilla flavouring*
3 *large cooking apples* *grated lemon rind*
3 *oz. sugar*

Add the rice slowly to the boiling water, then the peeled and chopped apples, sultanas, sugar, lemon rind and vanilla flavouring. Cook until the rice is tender, and serve either hot or cold, with whipped cream.

FRANKFURTER PUDDING
FRANKFURTER PUDDING

1 *oz. butter*	2 *oz. soft breadcrumbs*
2 *oz. sugar*	¼ *pint red wine*
4 *egg yolks*	2 *cloves*
4 *beaten egg whites*	*ground cinnamon*
½ *oz. blanched and chopped almonds*	*strip of lemon peel*

Cream the egg yolks and sugar together. Add the almonds, cinnamon and the breadcrumbs, previously dampened with a little wine. Beat well, then fold in the egg whites. Grease a pudding basin, sprinkle it with sugar and fill with the pudding mixture. Cover with a cloth and tie with string. Place the basin in a pan of boiling water, and keep on the boil for one hour.

Bring the rest of the wine to the boil with the lemon rind, simmer for a short while, and then serve as a thin sauce over the pudding.

MIXED FRUIT JELLY
FRUCHTSPEISE

½ *pint any kind of fruit purée*	¼ *pint whipped cream*
1 *oz. gelatine*	6 *oz. sugar*
2 *tablespoons lemon juice*	

Dissolve the gelatine. Cook the sugar with half a pint of water until you have a quarter of a pint of syrup. Add the gelatine and stir it well into the syrup before adding the purée. Beat all these ingredients together, add the

lemon juice and pour into a bowl. When the jelly has
almost set, whisk in the cream.

Pour into a rinsed mould and leave to set until firm.

WHIPPED CREAM
AND RASPBERRY SYRUP JELLY

SAFT-RAHMSPEISE

½ *pint whipped cream*   ½ *oz. gelatine*
1 *cup raspberry syrup*

Whisk the cream and syrup together, then add the
gelatine, previously dissolved. Leave in a cold place to
set.

BAKED APPLE AND RICE

APFELAUFLAUF MIT REIS

12 *peeled and chopped apples*   2 *beaten egg whites*
4 *oz. rice*   2 *oz. castor sugar*
½ *pint milk*   ½ *pint white wine or cider*
3 *oz. granulated sugar*   ½ *oz. butter*

Cook the apples in a little wine or cider until soft.
Drain, and arrange in the bottom of a buttered casserole. Bring the milk to the boil, add the rice and cook
with the granulated sugar and butter until soft. Cover
the apples with the rice. Beat the egg whites with the
castor sugar to a meringue consistency, then spread
over the rice.

Bake in a moderate oven until the meringue is a
golden brown.

ICED BOMBE
FÜRST PÜCKLER-RAHMBOMBE

Divide one pint of whipped cream into three portions. Colour one portion with cochineal or raspberry jelly, another with grated chocolate, adding maraschino. Flavour the third portion with cherry liqueur and mix with crushed macaroon biscuits.

Dissolve about one ounce of gelatine and add a third of it to each of the three portions.

Pour each portion separately into a tall glass mould. The macaroon portion first, then the raspberry and chocolate sections. Leave to set in a refrigerator until firm. Turn out and garnish with whipped cream and one large glacé cherry.

BAKED RICE PUDDING WITH APPLES
REISAUFLAUF

1 *pint milk*	2 *beaten egg whites*
3 *oz. rice*	2 *oz. sugar*
1 *lb. apples*	*rind of half a lemon*
2 *oz. butter*	*vanilla flavouring*
2 *egg yolks*	

Bring the milk with the lemon rind to the boil, then throw in the rice. Cook for five minutes. Draw to the side of the stove, cover with a cloth and a lid, and leave until the rice has absorbed all the milk. Remove the rind, and fold in the egg whites.

Cream the egg yolks and butter together, add the sugar and vanilla flavouring.

Peel, slice and parboil the apples. Arrange the apples and rice in alternate layers in a greased casserole, spread with the creamed egg and butter, and bake in a moderate oven for half an hour.

BAKED APPLE PUDDING
APFELAUFLAUF

2 *lb. cooking apples*	*grated rind of one lemon*
4 *oz. sugar*	3 *oz. blanched and chopped*
4 *oz. flour*	*almonds*
2 *eggs*	

Peel and slice the apples and arrange in the bottom of greased casserole. Sprinkle with sugar and almonds. Mix the eggs and the flour to a batter, and pour over the apples. Add the lemon juice and bake in a moderate oven until the apples are tender and the batter has set and browned.

COTTAGE CHEESE
AND STRAWBERRIES
QUARK MIT ERDBEEREN

½ *lb. cottage cheese*	*grated rind of half a lemon*
1 *lb. strawberries or raspberries*	3 *oz. sugar*
1 *cup whipped cream*	1 *teaspoon rum*

Rub the cheese through a sieve and mix with the cream. Add the lemon rind, rum and sugar. Arrange in a pile, pyramid shaped, and surround with strawberries. Serve with thin wafer biscuits.

APPLE PUREE

APFELMUSS

2 *lb. cooking apples*   1 *glass white wine or dry cider*
4 *oz. castor sugar*   *butter*

Peel, core and cut the apples into small pieces. Cook
with very little water and a small nob of butter. When
the apples are very soft, rub them through a sieve.
Add the sugar and the wine.

Serve chilled, and with whipped cream.

CHOCOLATE CREAM
WITH SNOWBALLS

SCHOKOLADENCREME MIT SCHNEEBÄLLEN

1 *pint milk*   2 *egg yolks*
2 *oz. sugar*   *Snowballs*:
1 *dessertspoon cornflour*   2 *egg whites*
4 *oz. grated chocolate*   2 *oz. castor sugar*

Mix the cornflour, chocolate and sugar in a little milk
to a thin paste. Beat the whites until stiff, then fold in
the castor sugar. Bring the milk to the boil, and drop
spoonfuls of the beaten egg whites into it. Poach for
three minutes. Remove with a draining spoon. Add the
cornflour paste to the milk, and cook until it thickens.
Remove from the fire. Gradually pour into the beaten
egg yolks, stirring all the time. Beat the cream until it is
cool, pour into a glass bowl, and when quite cold
garnish with the meringue snowballs.

APPLE FROMAGE
APFELCREME

2 *lb. cooking apples*   *sugar to taste*
1 *tablespoon lemon*   *grated lemon rind*
½ *cup whipped cream*

Peel and chop the apples and cook in a little water until
soft. Rub through a sieve, add the sugar and lemon
rind. Leave to cool, then fold in the whipped cream.
Serve with small macaroon biscuits.

Apricots, peaches, and rhubarb are also cooked in this
way.

RED BERRY CREAM
ROTE GRÜTZE

1 *lb. morello cherries*   4 *oz. sugar*
1 *lb. red currants*   1 *tablespoon cornflour*
1 *lb. raspberries*   1½ *pints water*

Clean the fruit. Bring the water to the boil, add the
fruit and sugar and cook until soft enough to rub
through a sieve. Return to the pan, reheat, and mix in
the cornflour (previously mixed with a little water).
Stir for three minutes. Pour into a glass bowl, cover and
leave to chill. Serve with whipped cream.

STEWED BILBERRIES
BLAUBEERENKOMPOTT

1 *lb. bilberries*   3 *oz. sugar*

Wash and pick over the bilberries, and sprinkle with

sugar. Put into a pan without water, and cook them gently for fifteen to twenty minutes.

A little lemon rind may be added while cooking and just a pinch of cinnamon.

To make a bilberry purée, cook the berries over a quick fire, then rub through a fine wire sieve. Mix with cream, and sugar, and a little light coloured honey.

APPLE SALAD

APFELSALAT

6 *large sweet apples*	3 *oz. icing sugar*
3 *oz. raisins*	*grated rind of one lemon*
3 *oz. ground hazel nuts*	½ *cup cream*
3 *oz. ground walnuts*	½ *cup milk*

Peel and slice the apples, then mix with the other ingredients.

Sliced peaches or apricots may be used in the same way.

PEACH AND PINEAPPLE SALAD

PFIRSICHSCHALE MIT ANANAS

6 *fresh peaches*	1 *glass Rhine wine*
6 *slices fresh pineapple*	4 *oz. granulated sugar*
1 *cup peeled and seeded grapes*	*icing sugar*

With a quarter of a pint of water and the granulated sugar make a syrup. Cool, and pour over the peaches. Leave for one hour. Cut the pineapple slices into halves, and arrange in a circle on a flat glass dish. Fill the centre with the peaches. Add the wine to the syrup and pour over the fruit. Garnish with the grapes, previously rolled in icing sugar. Chill before serving.

BANANAS WITH RUM

BANANENWASSER

Peel and cut 12 bananas into small pieces. Put them in a saucepan with just sufficient water to prevent burning. Flavour with plenty of lemon juice and sugar to taste. When the bananas are soft rub them through a sieve. Leave until cold, preferably in a refrigerator, then mix with rum just before serving.

GERMAN SWEET PASTRY
MÜRBETEIG

8 *oz. flour*	1 *egg*
4 *oz. butter*	1 *tablespoon rum or water*
1–2 *tablespoons sugar*	

Sift the flour in a mound on to a board and sprinkle with sugar. Flake the butter and rub it in the flour. Make a well in the centre of the flour, and drop the egg and rum (or water) into it. Work all the ingredients together with a spatula, beginning from the outside of the flour, and mix to a dough. Knead the dough until it is quite smooth. Cover with a bowl and let it stand in a cool place for one to two hours.

This type of pastry is used in Germany for open tarts, and biscuits or 'little bakings'.

Biscuits, or cookies, are a tradition with the German housewife, and she usually possesses dozens of differently-shaped pastry cutters to make her biscuits pretty and often quaint. Stars, half moons, and figures are favourite shapes. The biscuits are glazed with beaten egg before being baked, and often sprinkled with chopped nuts or decorated with cherries.

APPLE STRUDEL
APFELSTRUDEL

There are several ways of making Strudel pastry. Some cooks use a yeast pastry, others prefer a short pastry.

My recipe is the one more generally used, and was given me many years ago when a student in Germany by the cook in the German home where I was living. I still remember the large white kitchen table where, on a floured cloth, we stretched the pastry to get it thin enough to read a newspaper through it. Sometimes we made holes, and these Louise, the cook, carefully patched.

8 *oz. finely sieved white flour*   ¼ *pint warm water*
1½ *oz. melted butter*

Sift the flour in a mound on a large board, make a hollow in the middle and pour in the water. With a spatula blend the flour and water to a dough, working from the outside edges inwards. Add the melted butter, which must be cool. Knead the pastry well with both hands and beat it again and again on the board, until it is smooth and even slippery. Brush it with either warm oil or water, and leave it for half an hour on the board covered by a warm dish.

Put a large clean cloth, somewhat larger than a table napkin, on the table and flour it well. Roll out the dough on this cloth, as evenly and thinly as possible. Now slip your hands under the dough, lift it, and with the back of your hands gently pull it in all directions until it comes just beyond the edge of the cloth. This must be done very carefully, as I know from past experience that it is only too easy to tear the pastry. If you make tears, they must be patched with the odd pieces which you trim off the edges.

When the pastry is stretched to its fullest capacity spread first with melted butter, then with two tablespoons of fried breadcrumbs. Add one pound of peeled and chopped apples, two ounces of sugar, one ounce of blanched and chopped almonds, two ounces of sultanas or stoned raisins and a spoonful of ground cinnamon, and spread evenly. Lift up the edges of the cloth, and roll the Strudel evenly and tightly as you would a sponge roll. Brush the top with beaten egg or melted butter, and bake in a moderate oven until it is a golden brown colour. Sprinkle with castor sugar, and cut into thick slices when serving.

There are many fillings for Strudel pastry; the next two recipes are very popular.

CHERRY STRUDEL FILLING

KIRSCHSTRUDEL

Strudel pastry
1 oz. melted butter
2 tablespoons fried bread-
  crumbs

1 lb. cherries
3 oz. sugar
ground cinnamon

Stone the cherries, and partly cook them in very little water and some of the sugar. Spread the Strudel pastry with the melted butter and then with the remaining ingredients.

CURD CHEESE STRUDEL

KÄSESTRUDEL

Strudel pastry
1 oz. melted butter
2 tablespoons fried bread-
  crumbs

1 lb. curd or cottage cheese
2 beaten egg yolks
1 oz. sultanas
2 stiffly beaten egg whites

Brush the Strudel pastry with melted butter, then beat
the remainder of the ingredients together, and spread
evenly over the pastry.

BERLIN GARLAND CAKE-BREAD

BERLINER KRANZKUCHEN

1 *lb. flour*	½ *oz. yeast*
¼ *pint milk*	6 *oz. batter*
4 *eggs*	

For filling :

3 *oz. sweet almonds*	1 *teaspoon ground cinnamon*
3 *oz. sultanas*	1 *egg yolk*
3 *oz. currants*	20 *whole almonds*
2 *oz. candied peel*	*powdered sugar*
3 *oz. sugar*	

Slightly warm the milk and dissolve the yeast in it. Put
four ounces of flour into a bowl, make a well in the
centre and pour into it the dissolved yeast. Slowly stir
the flour into the yeast. Cover the bowl and leave the
batter to rise.

Blanch the sweet almonds and chop them into small
pieces. Clean the sultanas and currants. Chop the peel.
Add the remaining flour to the yeast mixture. Melt the
butter, let it cool then add it to the dough. Add the
eggs. Knead well and put onto a floured cloth. Roll the
paste into a long, thin sausage and divide into three.
Brush each piece with melted butter. Mix together the
currants, sultanas, chopped almonds, cinnamon and
peel and sprinkle these over the three pieces of dough.
Plait the three strips loosely together to allow for ex-

pansion. Brush once more with beaten egg yolk, join the ends of the plait together to form a garland and leave covered for three-quarters of an hour.

Blanch the 20 almonds and arrange these on the dough. Bake in a fairly hot oven until a pale, golden colour. When cold sprinkle with powdered sugar or a white, thin icing flavoured with a little rosewater.

CHRISTMAS BREAD

WEIHNACHTS STOLLEN

Stolle is the traditional Christmas bread in all parts of Germany. It is a cake-cum-fruit bread, and the most popular is the *Dresdner Stolle*.

3 *lb. flour*	4 *oz. chopped lemon rind*
½ *lb. suet*	4 *oz. chopped and blanched*
½ *lb. butter*	*almonds*
¾ *pint milk*	5 *beaten eggs*
3 *oz. sugar*	1 *oz. baker's yeast*
6 *oz. currants*	*pinch of salt*
6 *oz. raisins*	

Sift the flour into a warm bowl, make a well in the centre and pour in the yeast, first dissolved in a little warm milk. Add the eggs, salt, the rest of the milk and knead to a dough. Shred the butter and suet and gradually work it into the dough as you knead, and beat it until it blisters. Add currants, raisins and lemon rind, cover the bowl and leave to rise. Divide into two or three portions, and knead once more. Shape into long loaves. Leave once more to rise, this time to double its size. Put the loaves on a flat baking tin, and bake in a moderate oven for between fifty to sixty minutes. When

the loaves are ready, brush with hot melted butter and
dredge with sieved icing or castor sugar.

MACAROON TART
MAKRONENTORTE

8 oz. flour
3 oz. butter
1 oz. granulated sugar
1 egg yolk

6 oz. blanched and chopped
   almonds
2 oz. castor sugar
3 egg whites

From the flour, butter, egg yolk and sugar, make a
German sweet pastry and leave it to stand for thirty
minutes. Line a flan tin with the pastry, prick it with a
fork, and bake blind for five to ten minutes in a
moderate oven.

Grind the nuts. Beat the egg whites until stiff, fold
in the castor sugar, then add the nuts. Fill the flan case
with this mixture. Return to the oven and bake until
the pastry and the meringue are a golden brown.

WESTPHALIAN CHERRY FRUIT CAKE
WESTFALISCHER KIRSCHKUCHEN

5 oz. sieved flour
2 oz. butter
6 egg yolks
6 stiffly beaten egg whites

8 oz. sugar
5 oz. stale sponge crumbs
1 lb. stoned cherries

Prepare a German sweet pastry from the flour, butter,
one ounce of sugar and two egg yolks. Roll and fill a
flan tin. Bake in a hot oven for five to ten minutes. Beat
the remaining egg yolks and sugar together, fold in the
egg whites then add the crumbs.

Arrange the stoned cherries as close to each other as possible in the pastry case, and pour over them the sponge mixture. Bake in a moderate oven until the whole cake is a golden brown. Sprinkle with castor sugar when cooled.

APPLE CAKE

APFELKUCHEN

3 *lb. apples*
1 *lb. flour*
1 *gill warm milk*
3 *oz. butter*
grated lemon rind

1 *oz. sugar*
1–2 *eggs*
½ *oz. dry yeast*
pinch of salt
cinnamon

Dissolve the yeast in half the warm milk, adding a pinch of sugar. Sieve the flour into a warm bowl. Make a hollow in the centre, add the yeast, sprinkle with flour, and leave for thirty minutes in a warm place, covered with a cloth.

Warm the butter, mix with the sugar, salt, lemon rind, eggs and the rest of the milk, and add to the risen yeast pastry. Knead until the dough comes away from the sides of the bowl, and is a shining and smooth mass.

Dust with flour, cover, and leave once more to rise, and double its size.

Roll out the pastry quite thinly, and place on a large flat baking tin. Dredge with sugar or breadcrumbs. This is to prevent the fruit juice from soaking too much into the pastry.

Peel the apples, slice them thinly and completely cover the pastry. They should be arranged in rows each slice overlapping the other a little. Sprinkle with sugar and cinnamon. Bake in a moderate oven for twenty minutes or a little longer if necessary.

Plum tart is made in the same way, the plums being stoned and halved or even quartered and arranged very close together in rows. Brush with a fruit glaze or syrup.

POPPY SEED CAKE

MOHNTORTE

4 *oz. flour*   1 *tablespoon water*
3 *oz. butter*   1 *oz. sugar*
1 *egg*

From these ingredients make a sweet pastry and leave it to stand for half an hour under a damp cloth.

FOR THE FILLING:

5 *oz. poppy seed*   2 *oz. ground almonds*
3 *oz. sugar*   1 *oz. chopped peel (candied)*
2 *oz. ground chocolate* 1 *beaten egg*
2 *oz. stoned raisins*

As the poppy seed bought in England is not quite the same as that used in Germany, it is necessary to boil it first with a little milk. For five ounces of poppy seed you need four to five tablespoons of milk. Enough sugar is then mixed in to make a dry but soft consistency. Add the beaten egg, the rest of the sugar, almonds, peel, chocolate and raisins.

Roll the dough and cut into four layers of equal size. Line a flan tin with one layer and then spread with the poppy seed filling. Repeat this process with two more layers, but leave the top layer plain. Bake in a slow oven for one hour.

NUT CAKE
NUSSTORTE

1 *lb. ground walnuts*	3 *oz. breadcrumbs*
1 *whole egg*	¼ *pint milk*
2 *egg yolks*	1 *tablespoon rum*
2 *stiffly beaten egg whites*	1 *oz. sugar*

Soak the breadcrumbs in rum for a short while. Beat the whole egg and the two yolks together with sugar for half an hour. Add the breadcrumbs and the remaining ingredients, folding in the egg whites last of all. Grease a sponge cake tin with butter and fill it with the mixture, and bake for one hour. Carefully remove it from the tin and leave to cool. It can be eaten as it is, or cut into two layers and filled with a rich cream filling.

FILLING:

1 *cup of whipped cream*	1 *tablespoon rum*
3 *oz. sugar*	1 *teaspoon cornflour*
3 *oz. ground walnuts*	3 *egg yolks*

Heat, in a double boiler, the cream and the beaten egg yolks. Add the cornflour (previously mixed with a little of the cream to a paste) and stir the mixture until it is thick. Sprinkle in the walnuts, add the rum and continue stirring for a further two or three minutes. Take from the stove and whisk briskly until the cream is cold.

Spread the bottom layer of the cake with half of the filling. Replace the top layer, and spread this with the remaining filling and sprinkle freely with chopped nuts.

The main point to remember when making this cake is that it must be really well beaten, otherwise it will be extremely heavy.

It is very much a 'special' cake, and some recipes give as many as eleven eggs.

Hazel nuts may be used instead of walnuts and make an equally good cake.

CRUMBLE CAKE

STREUSELKUCHEN

This is a cake made with yeast, and liberally sprinkled with pastry crumbs.

FOR THE CAKE:

8 *oz. flour*	2 *eggs*
2 *oz. sugar*	½ *oz. baker's yeast*
2 *oz. butter*	1 *gill milk*

Dissolve the yeast in warm milk, and add one third of the flour to make a batter. Cover, and leave in a warm place to rise.

Cream the butter and sugar, add the eggs and the rest of the flour. Beat briskly, then work in the yeast batter. Knead the dough with the hands until it no longer sticks to the sides of the mixing bowl, then roll it out on a floured board. Prick it here and there to prevent blistering when baking. Re-roll and fill a shallow baking tin, brushing the top with melted butter.

TO MAKE THE CRUMBLE:

7 oz. flour   3 oz. sugar
2 oz. butter   1 teaspoon cinnamon

Melt the butter and while still hot mix with the sugar, flour and cinnamon. Cut the paste with a knife, then crumble like breadcrumbs.

Sprinkle the crumble over the rolled-out pastry, press it down lightly and then bake in a moderate oven until brown.

This type of cake is usually cut into squares, and the base when cooked should be about three-quarters of an inch high.

CHEESE OR CURD CAKE

KÄSEKUCHEN

Line a flan tin with pastry using the basic recipe for German sweet pastry.

FILLING:

5 egg yolks   5 beaten egg whites
5 oz. sugar   1 oz. currants
1 lb. cottage or curd cheese   grated rind of one lemon
1 tablespoon cornflour   vanilla essence

Cream the egg yolks and sugar, then add all the other ingredients, folding in the egg whites last of all. Fill the pastry case with this mixture and bake in a moderate oven for about forty-five minutes.

Serve cold. The flan should be about nine inches across and the filling at least one inch high.

LINZER TART
LINZERTORTE

2 oz. ground hazel nuts   8 oz. flour
2 eggs   grated lemon rind
3 oz. butter   red currant or raspberry jelly
3 oz. sugar

Cream the butter, sugar and eggs together. Add the flour, lemon rind and the nuts. Knead for thirty minutes. Break off three-quarters of the dough and roll into a round about nine inches across and one inch high. Take a plate which is about eight inches across and press into the round until you have an indentation of about half an inch. Put the pastry in a flan tin, and spread it evenly with the jam. Roll out the remaining pastry thinly and cut into strips. Weave the strips of pastry across the top to form a lattice. Bake in a medium oven for one hour.

CHESTNUT CAKE
KASTANIENTORTE

3 oz. flour   8 oz. chestnuts
5 egg yolks   ½ pint whipped cream
5 beaten egg whites   6 oz. sugar
5 oz. butter   vanilla essence

Bake the chestnuts until you can remove the outer shell and the brown skin inside. Boil them until they are soft enough to pass through a potato ricer. Cream the butter, sugar and egg yolk, and flavour with essence. Add the mashed chestnuts, flour, and lastly fold in the egg whites.

Grease a cake tin (one with a loose bottom or spring side) and dredge with a few breadcrumbs. Fill with the chestnut mixture. Cook in a moderate oven until brown.

Beat the cream with a little sugar and a little coffee colouring and spread over the cake when cold.

Some German cooks prefer to slice the cake into two layers and fill with whipped cream.

SACHER TORTE
SACHERTORTE

5 *oz. butter*	5 *stiffly beaten egg whites*
5 *oz. sugar*	5 *oz. grated chocolate*
5 *oz. flour*	2 *tablespoons apricot jam*
5 *egg yolks*	*chocolate icing*

Cream the butter and sugar together, then add the flour and the egg yolks alternately. Beat well. Add the grated chocolate and fold in the egg whites. Bake in a medium oven until brown.

When the cake is cold, slice it through and spread the lower half with apricot jam. Replace the top half and spread this with chocolate icing.

Some cooks leave the cake for two days before cutting and icing. Instead of using icing, the top can be spread with whipped cream and sprinkled with very coarsely ground nuts.

This is strictly speaking a Viennese speciality, but has been adopted largely by the Germans. It was one of the many culinary inventions of Madame Sacher, wife of the famous Viennese chêf and hotelier.

SANDCAKE

SANDTORTE

A very dry and crumbly kind of cake very popular throughout Germany and neighbouring countries as well.

½ *lb. butter*   4 *egg yolks*
½ *lb. sugar*   4 *stiffly beaten egg whites*
½ *lb. potato flour*   1 *liqueur glass of rum*

Beat the butter for twenty minutes until it becomes creamy. Add the sugar, then one by one the egg yolks. Continue beating for one hour. As you beat gradually add the rest of the ingredients, lastly folding in the egg whites. Pour this mixture into a deep round greased cake tin, and bake for one hour in a moderate oven.

Some recipes suggest that less baking makes for a better though underdone cake. It is important to have the cake tin well greased before the cake is made, for immediately you cease beating the tin must be filled.

FRUIT CAKE

NAPFKUCHEN

This cake is baked in an angel cake form, that is a deep round cake tin with a large 'cone' in the middle.

6 *oz. butter*   1 *lb. sieved flour*
7 *oz. sugar*   2 *oz. sultanas*
3 *eggs*   2 *oz. candied peel*
¼ *pint milk*   2 *oz. currants*
1 *oz. almonds*   1 *oz. baking powder*

Wash and dry the currants and sultanas. Blanch and chop the almonds, and cut the candied peel into thin strips.

Cream the butter and sugar together, and add the eggs one by one. Continue beating, adding at the same time the currants, sultanas, flour, baking powder, peel, almonds and the milk. Pour into a well-greased angel cake tin and bake in a moderate oven until it is brown.

CHRISTMAS FRITTERS
WEIHNACHTS SCHÜRZKUCHEN

3 *oz. butter*   3 *tablespoons water*
3 *oz. sugar*   1 *lb. flour*
3 *eggs*   1 *teaspoon baking powder*
3 *tablespoons milk*

Cream the butter and sugar together. Add the other ingredients, and beat to a dough with a wooden spoon. Knead well with the hands, and chill.

Turn the dough on to a floured board and roll out very thinly. With a pastry wheel or very sharp knife cut strips three inches long and three-quarters of an inch wide. In the middle of each strip cut a gash, and twist the ends through. Fry in deep hot fat until a golden brown. Drain on absorbent paper, dust with sieved icing or castor sugar.

BUTTER CAKES
BUTTERKRINGEL

4 *oz. butter*   2 *egg whites*
6 *oz. flour*   *pinch of salt*
4 *oz. sugar*   *vanilla flavouring*
3 *egg yolks*

These are very light tea cakes or biscuits, rather better described by the American term 'cookies'.

Beat the butter and the yolks to a cream then gradually add flour and sugar, beating vigorously all the time. Add the salt and the vanilla flavouring—the amount depends on personal taste. Beat the egg whites until fairly stiff but not dry. Fold these into the mixture. Push the mixture through a large piper and describe either circles or the letter 'S' on a floured, flat baking sheet. Bake in a medium oven until a light brown.

'BLITZ' CAKES
BLITZKUCHEN

These should take only five minutes to bake.

4 *oz. flour*   4 *oz. sugar*
4 *oz. butter*   4 *eggs*

Beat the butter until it is creamy, then gradually add the eggs, sugar and flour, beating vigorously all the time. Pour the mixture on to the greased baking tin—it should be a little warm before using—smoothing it out so there is a thin equal layer. Put the tin into a hot oven and bake for five minutes. While still hot cut the cake into long, thin lengths using a sharp knife.

WHITE GINGER NUTS

WEISSE PFEFFERNÜSSE

8 oz. flour	2 oz. grated lemon rind
6 oz. sugar	¼ teaspoon ground ginger
1 teaspoon baking powder	½ teaspoon ground nutmeg
2 eggs	1 teaspoon ground cloves

Cream the eggs and sugar together, then add the spices, ginger, lemon rind, sieved flour and baking powder. Mix to a dough, and knead with the hands until it is firm and smooth. Shape into a long roll, cut into quarter inch thick slices, and bake on a greased and floured baking sheet.

Keep for twenty-four hours before using.

NUREMBURG GINGER NUTS

NÜRNBERGER BRAUNE LEBKUCHEN

¾ lb. honey	3 oz. candied orange peel
6 oz. sugar	3 oz. candied lemon peel
1½ lb. flour	½ teaspoon ground cloves
pinch of baking soda	½ teaspoon ground cinnamon
1 teaspoon baking powder	½ teaspoon ground ginger
½ lb. chopped almonds	

Bring the honey, with half the sugar, to boiling point, and keep boiling until it drops in beads from the spoon. Leave to cool, then pour it over the sieved flour. Add the baking powder and the soda. Knead to a smooth dough and leave for two days.

Boil the remaining sugar with a little water to a syrup. Quickly sauté the almonds in this.

Blend the syrup and almonds into the dough as quickly as possible, adding the spices and ginger. Roll out the dough on to a floured board. Cut with a sharp knife, sprinkle with the peel (chopped) and leave in a warm place until next day.

Bake in a hot oven and while still warm brush with a sugar glaze.

MARBLE CAKE

MARMORKUCHEN

½ lb. butter	3 oz. potato flour
½ lb. sugar	1 teaspoon baking powder
4 eggs	salt and vanilla essence
¼ pint milk	1 tablespoon milk
2 oz. grated chocolate	about 8 bitter almonds
12 oz. sieved flour	

Cream the butter, sugar and eggs together. Add the salt, vanilla essence, flour, potato flour, milk and baking powder. Beat well to a smooth, soft consistency.

Grind the almonds, and mix with the grated chocolate and milk to a paste.

Divide the cake mixture into two portions, and mix one portion with the chocolate paste. Pour the white portion into an oblong greased cake tin, or an angel-cake tin, reserving one third. Add the chocolate portion, then the remaining white mixture. Bake in a moderate oven for about one hour.

HAZEL NUT MACAROONS
HAZELNUSS-MANDELMAKRONEN

4 *egg whites*   6 *oz. hazel nuts*
6 *oz. castor sugar*   2 *oz. almonds*

Beat the egg whites until they are stiff and fold in the
sugar. Grind the nuts (without blanching) very finely,
and add to the egg whites. Drop in teaspoonfuls on to
a greased baking sheet and bake in a moderate oven
until they are a pale golden colour. Decorate with
strips of candied peel or glacé cherries before putting
in the oven.

ALMOND PASTE
LÜBECKER MARZIPAN
A Lübeck recipe

Although it is possible to buy Lübecker marzipan all
the year round, it is especially part of the Christmas
tradition, when the makers shape the marzipan into
the most delightfully realistic looking animal figures or
fruits.

1 *lb. almonds*   *orangewater (or rosewater)*
1 *lb. sieved icing sugar*

Blanch the almonds and dry carefully. Grind them very
finely, and mix with the icing sugar. Work into a firm
paste, adding just enough orange water to make it
pliable.

Put the marzipan into a pan and stir over a low heat
until it no longer sticks to the sides of the pan.

Turn out on to a sugar-dusted board, and shape into figures. Put into a warm oven and leave there long enough to dry, but watch that the marzipan remains both white and soft.

CHRISTMAS TREE BISCUITS
CHRISTBAUMGEBÄCK

1 *lb. flour*   ½ *lb. sugar*   4 *eggs*

Cream the eggs and sugar for ten to fifteen minutes. Add the flour. Roll out the dough on a floured board, and cut with pastry cutters into quaint shapes. Tiny figures, stars, and rings are the usual varieties.

Brush with beaten egg yolk, and bake in a hot oven.

As these biscuits are mainly for children, they are frequently glazed with coloured icing, then tied with Christmas string and hung on the Christmas tree.

CINNAMON STARS
ZIMT STERNE

4 *beaten egg whites*   12 *blanched almonds*
8 *oz. castor sugar*   1 *teaspoon cinnamon*

Grind the almonds very finely, mix with the sugar and cinnamon, and work to a paste, then gradually add the egg whites. Drop teaspoonfuls of the mixture on to a board dusted with icing sugar, decorate with strips of candied peel, or glacé cherries, and bake in a moderate oven until a pale golden colour.

FRANKFURTER FIGURES
FRANKFURTER BRENTON

1 *lb. almonds*
1 *lb. sugar*
2 *oz. flour*

3–4 *tablespoons rosewater*
1 *egg white*

Blanch the almonds and pound in a mortar. Add the rosewater and the sugar, and cook over a very low fire until the mixture no longer sticks to the sides of the pan. Put the almond paste in a sugar-dusted bowl, cover with a cloth and leave until next day.

Sieve the flour and work it into the paste. Add the egg white, slightly beaten, and knead until it is smooth. Shape into fat figures, which look as if they are cut out of wood. Cover once more and leave for a further twenty-four hours. Bake on a greased baking sheet for about thirty minutes.

These Frankfurter Figures are said to have been great favourites with the German poet, Goethe, who was born in Frankfurt.

ALMOND BRETZELS
MANDEL-BRETZELN

8 *oz. flour*
½ *lb. ground almonds*

4 *oz. butter*
2 *eggs*

Cream the butter and eggs together. Add the flour and almonds. Roll out with the rolling pin, then cut into strips. Each strip should be about six inches long, and rounded with the hands. Tie the strips into a bow or lover's knot. Brush with beaten egg and bake in a medium oven until they are a golden brown.

SALT AND CARRAWAY STICKS
SALZ UND KÜMMELSTANGEN

½ *lb. flour*
4 *oz. butter*
4 *tablespoons cream*

1 *egg yolk*
salt
carraway seeds

Cream the butter, add the cream and flour and mix to a firm dough. Knead well, and roll out thinly. Cut into strips, brush with egg, sprinkle with salt and carraway seeds, and bake in a moderate oven until a golden brown.

NUT FRITTERS
NUSS KRAPFEN

4 oz. butter
6 oz. sugar
4 oz. chopped walnuts
4 beaten eggs

1 lb. flour
1 dessertspoon baking powder
ground cinnamon
milk for mixing

Cream the butter and sugar together, then add the beaten eggs. Gradually work in the flour, cinnamon, baking powder, and walnuts. Knead to a dough. Roll out, cut into strips, and shape into stars, triangles, and other shapes. Fry in deep fat and sprinkle with sugar.

JAM DOUGHNUTS
BERLINER PFANNKUCHEN

1 lb. flour
½ oz. baker's yeast
1 gill warm milk
3 oz. sugar

2 beaten eggs
pinch of salt
2 oz. melted butter

Dissolve the yeast in the milk, then mix with four ounces of flour. Stand in a bowl in a warm place, and leave to rise. Add the butter, the eggs, salt, and the rest of the flour, and beat to a soft smooth dough. Leave once more to rise double its size. Turn on to a floured board, and break off small pieces. Roll each piece flat. Put a little jam in the centre of one piece, then cover with another, pinching the edges firmly. Repeat until all the dough is used up. Leave again to rise. Drop into deep boiling fat. Fry for about two minutes on one side, then turn and fry the other side. Remove with a draining spoon and turn on to paper to drain off the surplus fat. Roll in castor sugar and serve while still warm.

These are traditionally eaten on New Year's Eve, and are served with hot punch.

HOUSEWIFE FRITTERS
HAUSFRAUEN KRAPFEN

Mix together some cold left-over rice and soft fruit, and bind with a beaten egg. Break off pieces, shape into balls, and fry in deep boiling fat.

Serve with stewed fruit or a fruit sauce.

THE JOLLY SPINSTERS (Fritters)
FRÖHLICHE JUNGFRAUEN

2 oz. sugar	*2 oz. cornflour*
4 eggs	*grated rind of one lemon*
2 tablespoons flour	

Beat the yolks of the eggs together with the sugar and lemon rind until they are creamy. Add the flour and cornflour, then the egg whites beaten stiffly. Drop spoonfuls of this mixture into boiling fat. Cook for a few minutes until the fritters are a golden brown, strain off surplus fat on to absorbent paper, and serve with a wine sauce.

SNOWBALLS

SCHNEEBÄLLE

1 *oz. butter*	*vanilla essence*
4 *oz. flour*	*grated lemon rind*
3 *eggs*	2 *oz. sugar*

Bring the butter to the boil with about one gill of water, then add the flour, sugar, lemon rind and flavouring. Stir vigorously. Remove from the stove. Drop in the eggs, one after the other, making sure that each egg is thoroughly worked into the dough before adding another. Break off pieces, shape into balls, and drop into boiling fat. Fry on both sides until brown.

Roll in castor or icing sugar.

These can be split into two and filled with whipped cream.

The following five recipes are for various ways of frying bread. Milk bread is the best type to use, but ordinary white bread or even split buns will do.

POOR KNIGHTS

ARME RITTER

4 *slices of bread*	*sugar*
1 *egg*	*cinnamon*
milk	*salt*

Soak the bread in milk for fifteen minutes. Beat the egg, add a small pinch of salt, then dip the soaked bread into the egg. Take out with a cooking slice and coat with breadcrumbs. Fry in hot fat on both sides. Mix sugar and ground cinnamon to taste and sprinkle on each slice of bread. Serve hot.

BREAD FRITTERS
GEBACKENE BROTSCHNITTEN

slices of white bread   *milk*
egg batter

Soak the bread in milk for fifteen minutes, then drop
into the batter. Fry in hot fat, and serve with lemon
juice and sugar or apricot jam.

GOLD SLICES
GOLDSCHNITTEN

slices of white bread   *2 beaten eggs*
3 oz. ground almonds   *1 oz. sugar*

Leave the slices of bread in the milk only long enough
to soak through, and no longer. Coat with ground
almonds, sprinkle with sugar then dip in the beaten
eggs, making sure that they are well covered. Fry in
deep hot fat, and sprinkle when serving with sugar and
ground cinnamon.

STRAWBERRY SLICES
ERDBEERSCHNITTEN

slices of white bread   *strawberries*
sugar

Fry the bread on one side only in butter until crisp.
While still hot, cover the uncooked side with strawberries and sprinkle with castor sugar. Add cream when
serving.
    Almost any fruit can be served in this way.

WINE SLICES
WEINSCHNITTEN

6 *white bread slices*   2 *eggs*
red wine   *sugar and cinnamon*

The eggs and wine must be beaten to a smooth liquid,
in which to soak the bread. Leave until the liquid has
been quite absorbed by the bread. Fry in deep fat,
and sprinkle with sugar and cinnamon. Serve with a
hot wine sauce, or spread the slices with apricot jam
and a fruit sauce.

BAKING POWDER DOUGHNUTS
BACKPULVER KRAPFEN

4 *eggs*   1 *lb. flour*
½ *pint milk*   1 *dessertspoon baking powder*

Beat the eggs and milk together. Add the baking
powder to the flour, then mix all the ingredients together to make a dough. Drop spoonfuls into deep
boiling fat. Fry to a light golden brown. Remove with
draining spoon on to paper to absorb the surplus fat.
Roll in castor sugar and serve with a fruit sauce.

NOODLES
NUDELN

MOST British housewives prefer to buy noodles ready made. They can, however, be made at home.

6 *oz. flour*   2 *egg yolks*   *salt*

Sift the flour on to a floured board, and make a well in the centre. Drop the yolks into the well, add a pinch of salt, and with a spatula, work into a very stiff dough. If the dough is not very stiff, add a little more flour. Knead slightly. Roll out evenly and paper thin, cover with a cloth and leave for fifteen minutes. Cut into lengths, separate, dry and leave stored in a covered jar until needed.

GIPSY NOODLES
ZIGEUNERNUDELN

Stew about one pound of plums in very little water. Flavour with cinnamon and lemon juice. Rub through a sieve.

Cook in a large pan of boiling salted water about half a pound of noodles until tender. Strain and arrange in a well-greased casserole. Stir in the plum purée, and bake in a hot oven for ten minutes. Serve sprinkled with coarse brown sugar.

BAKED NOODLES
SÜSSER NUDELAUFLAUF

4 oz. noodles	1 tablespoon currants
1 lb. cooked apples	1 egg
1 lb. cooked pears	1 teaspoon grated lemon rind
3 oz. sugar	ground cinnamon
	breadcrumbs

Cook the noodles in boiling salted water until tender.
Strain, and with the fruit, arrange in alternate layers
in a greased casserole. The top layer should be of apples.

Beat the egg in about quarter of a pint of fruit juice.
Sweeten to taste, flavour with cinnamon, and pour over
the apples.

Cover with breadcrumbs and sprinkle with lemon
rind. Dot with butter and bake in a moderate oven for
about twenty minutes.

NOODLE MERINGUE PIE
NUDELAUFLAUF MIT EIERSCHAUMDECKE

4 oz. noodles	1 teaspoon grated lemon rind
1 oz. butter	and juice
2 egg yolks	4 tablespoons jam
2 beaten egg whites	ground cinnamon
3 oz. sugar	

Cook the noodles in boiling milk with a pinch of salt
and the butter, until they are tender. Cool. Beat the
yolks with about one half of the sugar, and stir into the
noodles. Put the noodles into a greased casserole, add

the jam, flavouring it first with a little lemon juice, the cinnamon and the lemon rind.

Beat the egg whites, with the remainder of the sugar, until stiff. Spread over the mixture.

Bake until the meringue cover is a pale golden colour.

BREAD
BROT

RYE BREAD
ROGGENBROT

1 *lb. rye flour*
4 *oz. white flour*
½ *oz. baker's yeast*
1 *pint milk*

1 *teaspoon salt*
2 *teaspoons pounded aniseed
or fennel*

Dissolve the yeast in warm milk, and mix with four ounces of the rye flour. Leave to rise overnight.

Next day, add the rest of the ingredients, and knead smoothly. Put into a warm bowl, cover with a cloth and leave in a warm place to rise until it has doubled its bulk.

Shape into two loaves, put on a greased baking sheet, and bake in a moderate oven for thirty minutes. Brush with warm water, return to the oven and continue baking for another hour and fifteen minutes.

BLACK BREAD
SCHWARZBROT

1½ *lb. rye flour*
1 *pint warm milk*

1 *teaspoon salt*
1 *oz. baker's yeast*

Dissolve the yeast in a little of the warm milk, add a little of the flour and leave to rise. Add the other ingredients and once more leave to rise until it has doubled its bulk. Bake for two hours in a slow oven.

The Germans also use a 'sour dough' method of baking bread. Mix two tablespoons of flour with enough water to make a thick paste. Leave this paste in a warm place, and in a stone jar for six days. Thin the paste with a little water and use it in exactly the same way that you do yeast.

Those German housewives who frequently make their own bread, always reserve about one tablespoonful of the mixture, cover with water and keep it for up to eight days, when they are ready for another baking day.

COFFEE BREAD

KAFFEEKUCHEN

4 *oz. melted butter*	½ *pint lukewarm milk*
1½ *lb. white flour*	1 *beaten egg*
½ *oz. baker's yeast*	2 *oz. sugar*
1 *beaten egg*	¼ *teaspoon carraway seeds*

Dissolve the yeast in a little warm milk and about four ounces of flour. Leave to stand overnight.

Next day mix the remaining milk, sugar, egg, and flour to a pliable dough. Add yeast and the butter, and beat with a wooden spoon until smooth and firm. Leave covered with a cloth in a warm place for two hours.

To shape the coffee bread, divide the dough in two parts and cut each into two or three. Roll each piece with the hands into long rolls or braids, and plait. Place on a greased baking sheet, brush each loaf with egg and water, and sprinkle with carraway seeds. Bake in a moderate oven for about thirty to forty minutes.

These loaves can, of course, be made without plait-
ing, and in loaf tins.

CAKE BREAD
KUCHENBROT

1 *lb. white flour*   1 *teaspoon grated lemon rind*
½ *oz. baker's yeast*   1½ *oz. butter*
¼ *pint lukewarm milk*   3 *oz. sultanas or raisins*
1 *oz. sugar*

Dissolve the yeast in a little milk, then add about three
ounces of flour. Leave to rise in a warm place. Add the
other ingredients, and beat to a firm but smooth dough.
Place in a large warm bowl, cover with a cloth and
leave to rise until it has doubled its size.

Half fill two tins with the dough, leave to rise until it
reaches the top of the tins, put into a cold oven, and
bake for one and a half hours, allowing the oven to
reach a temperature of 350° F.

MERINGUE BREAD
KLEZENBROT

5 *oz. flour*   7 *oz. almonds*
8 *oz. sugar*   6 *oz. sultanas*
4 *beaten egg whites*   1½ *oz. chopped candied peel*

Beat the sugar into the egg whites, and continue beating
for twenty minutes. Add the almonds, sultanas and
peel, lastly the flour. Cover a greased baking sheet

with greaseproof paper, spread the mixture on the sheet and bake in a warm oven until pale golden colour.

Cut the meringue bread into pieces about three inches long, and half an inch across. This type of bread is served with stewed fruit.

A PUNCH or wine cup should bring pleasure and not a hangover. Only good wine, or good champagne should be used, and unspoiled fruit. Sugar must be used sparingly, and as a general rule mineral waters and bottled fruit juices avoided. Always cool on ice. Serve with small home-made sweet biscuits.

EGG NOGG I
EIER PUNSCH I

4 eggs
4 egg yolks
2 oz. sugar

10 tablespoons rum
1 tablespoon lemon juice
¼ pint water

Cream the eggs and the sugar together, then stir over a low heat with the rest of the ingredients until the mixture becomes thick and frothy.

EGG NOGG II
EIER PUNSCH II

2 bottles red wine
½ lb. brown sugar
1 pint water
juice of one orange
juice of one lemon

1 cup tea (milkless)
1 wineglass rum
10 eggs
nutmeg, cloves

Boil the water with the nutmeg, cloves, sugar until the liquid is reduced to one third of its original quantity.

Strain, and return to the pan, adding the juices and the tea. Beat the eggs to a cream and stir into the wine. Pour this into the spiced water, return to the fire, and, stirring all the time, bring almost to boiling point. Serve hot.

BISHOP'S PUNCH I
BISCHOF PUNSCH I

1 *bottle white Rhine wine*   4 *oz. sliced fresh pineapple*
1 *bottle sparkling wine*   1 *tot rum*
1 *glass madeira*   *sugar to taste*
1 *coffee spoon curaçao*

Put the pineapple at the bottom of a punch bowl, and cover with Rhine wine. Leave for six hours. Add the other ingredients, pouring in the sparkling wine last.

BISHOP'S PUNCH II
BISCHOF PUNSCH II

3 *oz. sugar*   1 *tablespoon curaçao*
1 *bottle red wine*

Stir the sugar with quarter of a pint of water until it melts. Add the wine and the curaçao.

CARDINAL PUNCH I
KARDINAL PUNSCH I

1 *bottle white Rhine wine*   4 *oz. chopped fresh pineapple*
8 *oz. sugar*   ½ *bottle champagne*

Arrange the pineapple in a punch bowl, sprinkle with sugar, then pour in the wine. Put on ice, and leave for one hour before adding the champagne.

CARDINAL PUNCH II
KARDINAL PUNSCH II

1 *bottle red wine*
1 *lb. sugar*

juice and peel of 4 oranges
4 whole oranges

Melt the sugar in a saucepan with as little water as possible. Add the wine, orange juice and peel. Stir, and bring to almost boiling point, then take from the fire, strain and leave to cool.

Slice the whole oranges, without peeling, and drop them into the punch while it is still warm.

Chill before serving.

BERLIN PUNCH
BERLINER PUNSCH

1 *bottle sparkling wine*
1 *teaspoon lemon juice*

sugar to taste
2 bottles Berlin white beer

Stir all the ingredients together in a bowl.

HOT MILK PUNCH
HEISSEMILCHPUNSCH

1 *pint of milk*
½ *pint rum*
2 *egg yolks*

lemon peel
vanilla bean
sugar to taste

Bring the milk to the boil with the lemon rind and vanilla bean. Strain. Beat the egg with the sugar and the rum, then pour into the still hot milk, stirring all the while. Re-heat, but do not boil. Serve very hot.

NEW YEAR'S PUNCH
NEUJAHRSPUNSCH

2 *bottles white wine*	½ *bottle rum*
½ *bottle red wine*	½ *lb. soft sugar*

Dissolve the sugar in the rum and leave for several hours. Bring the wine almost to the boil, then add the sweetened rum and serve at once.

CHAMPAGNE CUP
SEKTBOWLE

Slice some apples, bananas, fresh peaches, apricots and strawberries. Arrange in a bowl, and dredge with icing sugar. Add a bottle of champagne.

PINEAPPLE WINE CUP
ANANASBOWLE

½ *a chopped fresh pineapple*	4–5 *oz. sugar*
2 *bottles Moselle wine*	1 *bottle seltzer (soda water)*
½ *bottle sparkling wine*	

Put the fruit into a bowl and lightly dredge with sugar. Pour over it two or three glasses of the Moselle wine, and leave standing for several hours. Cool the remain-

der of the wine, and add to the fruit just before serving.
The soda water is added at the last minute.

ROSEPETAL WINE CUP
ROSENBOWLE

1 *bottle Vichy water*   1 *bottle dry white wine*
1 *bottle sparkling wine*   *a small bowlful fresh rose petals*
3 *bottles sweet white wine*   6 *oz. icing sugar*

Cabbage rose petals are the best type for this recipe.
Pile the petals in a deep bowl, and dredge with icing
sugar. Leave for twenty minutes, then cover with
Vichy water. Leave on ice for one hour. Strain through
a muslin bag, and mix thoroughly with the other ingredients. Serve at once while the perfume of the petals
is still strong.

There is also an old German recipe for this cup which
has a suggestion of the Orient. In this recipe the rose
petals are first crushed, then covered with a syrup and
soaked in Rhine wine for forty minutes. You then
strain them, and add one or two drops of cochineal,
and three or four drops of rosewater.

When serving either type of cup, put one fresh petal
into each glass.

MIGNONETTE WINE CUP
RESEDABOWLE

1 *large handful mignonette*   1 *bottle sparkling wine*
  flowers   1 *bottle red wine*
2 *bottles white wine*   6 *oz. sugar*

Tie up the flowers in a muslin bag and leave them for one hour in a basin in half a bottle of red wine. Squeeze the bag well to obtain all the mignonette flavour. Mix all the ingredients together. Serve immediately, otherwise the cup loses its unusual flavour.

Lime flowers, and grape vine blossoms are also used in this way.

RUM PUNCH

RUMPUNSCH

½ *bottle rum*   1 *orange*
½ *bottle red wine*   4 *tablespoons pineapple juice*
½ *bottle white wine*   ¾ *pint water*
5 *oz. sugar*

Bring the rum, sugar, wine, pineapple juice and water almost to the boil. Slice the orange, put it into a punch bowl and pour in the hot punch.

Serve at once.

MULLED WINE I

GLÜHWEIN I

1 *bottle red wine*   2 *cloves*
¼ *pint water*   1 *inch of cinnamon stick*
½ *lb. sugar*   *lemon peel*

Boil all the ingredients, except the wine, and reduce the quantity by half. Strain, add to the wine, and bring almost to boiling point.

Serve hot.

MULLED WINE II
GLÜHWEIN II

6 *bottles red wine*	2 *lb. soft brown sugar*
3 *bottles water*	1 *lemon and* 1 *orange*
½ *stick of cinnamon*	*about* 20 *cloves*

Stick the cloves into the lemon and orange and roast in the oven until the fruit juice begins to ooze. Bring the water to the boil with the cinnamon, the roasted orange and lemon. Continue boiling until the water has been reduced to quarter the original amount. Strain, add to the wine, and bring almost to boiling point. Serve hot.

WOODRUFF WINE BOWL
WALDMEISTERBOWLE

Carefully pluck the young woodruff blossoms before they are in full bloom, and put them into a muslin bag. To one bottle of Moselle wine use three ounces of sugar. Pour into a bowl and hang the bag of woodruff in the wine and leave for ten minutes. Chill, and place one thin slice of orange in the bowl before serving.

This is a famous German cup.

STRAWBERRY CUP
ERDBEERBOWLE

1 *lb. fresh strawberries*	1 *bottle sparkling wine*
2 *bottles light white wine*	5 *oz. sugar*

Hull the strawberries, but do not wash unless absolutely necessary. Put them into a bowl, dredge with sugar and leave for one hour. Add first the white wine, then the sparkling.

Serve chilled.

CUCUMBER CUP

GURKENBOWLE

1 *bottle red wine*	1 *sprig borage*
½ *bottle sherry*	1 *cucumber*
1 *bottle Vichy water*	1 *liqueur glass curaçao*
1 *thinly sliced orange*	*icing sugar*

Slice the cucumber very finely and arrange at the bottom of a bowl. Add the orange and the bruised borage. Dredge with sugar, pour in the curaçao, and leave for twenty minutes. Pour in the wine, sherry and Vichy water. Leave on ice for fifteen minutes and serve well chilled.

Melon may be used instead of cucumber.

ICED COFFEE WITH WHIPPED CREAM
EISKAFFEE I

¼ *pint water*
¼ *pint freshly made coffee*

½ *pint thick or whipped cream*
sugar to taste

Boil the water and the sugar together then add the coffee. Cool, add the cream, and chill in the refrigerator.

To make a chocolate iced drink omit coffee and use grated chocolate.

VANILLA ICE COFFEE
EISKAFFEE II

about 8 *tablespoons strong black coffee*
whipped cream

1 *heaped tablespoon vanilla ice cream*

Put the ice cream into a tall glass and pour the coffee over it. Top with whipped cream.

ALMOND MILK
MANDELMILCH

To one pint of milk add four ounces of ground almonds, put in the refrigerator for several hours, and pour through a sieve before serving.

FRUIT JUICE SODA MILK

SAFT, ZITRONE, SELTER, MILCH

about 8 *tablespoons raspberry*
  juice
juice of four lemons

bottle soda water
1 *pint milk*

Stir all together, adding the soda water last, and chill before serving.

This drink can be made with orange juice instead of lemons, or by omitting the raspberry juice and sweetening with icing sugar.

Fresh fruit juice is usually prepared by the German housewife herself.

HERBAL TEAS

The Germans are great herbal tea-drinkers, and can usually produce a herbal cure for all ills.

APPLE TEA

APFELTEE

Pour half a pint of boiling water over a handful of apple peelings. Leave to steep until the water becomes brown. Strain.

Used as blood purifier and mild laxative.

NETTLE TEA

BRENNESSELTEE

Pour boiling water over some nettles, strain and drink while still hot. For aches and pains generally.

LIME TEA
LINDENBLÜTENTEE

Boil the lime flowers in water, about a teaspoonful to a half pint of water, and strain.

For nerves, catarrh, colds and coughs. Also slimming.

VALERIAN TEA
BALDRIANTEE

Pour a quarter of a pint of water over quarter of an ounce of valerian leaves and leave to draw for twelve hours. Strain. A mild sedative.

VANILLA SUGAR
VANILLEZUCKER

1 *vanilla bean*　　　　　　1 *lb. sugar*

Cut the bean into several pieces and put with the sugar into a tightly-covered glass jar. Leave for several weeks before opening. The sugar will have a delightful flavour of vanilla, and the pieces of bean can be used again and again.

LEMON SUGAR
ZITRONENZUCKER

Grate the rind of one lemon and mix it with one pound of sugar. Put in a covered jar and use as required.

ROSE SUGAR

ROSENZUCKER

Put the sugar on to a plate and sprinkle with a few
drops of rose water. Allow the sugar to dry, then put
into a covered jar and use as required.

INDEX

INDEX